CROSSCURRENTS *Modern Critiques*

CROSSCURRENTS *Modern Critiques*
Harry T. Moore, *General Editor*

Sergio Pacifici

The Modern Italian Novel

FROM MANZONI TO SVEVO

WITH A PREFACE BY
Harry T. Moore

Carbondale and Edwardsville

SOUTHERN ILLINOIS UNIVERSITY PRESS

FEFFER & SIMONS, INC.

London and Amsterdam

For my wife, Jeanne,
"qui remplit mon cœur de clarté"
and for my daughters, Tina and Sabrina,
with much love

PREFACE

SERGIO PACIFICI'S BOOK is essentially a history of the nine-teenth-century Italian novel. Professor Pacifici, who teaches at Queens College of the City University of New York, points out in his Introduction that there has been no his-tory of the Italian novel since Domenico Vittorini's, "pub-lished three and one-half decades ago." The passing of time has brought changes in perspective and shifts in em-phasis, hence it is good to have Mr. Pacifici's up-to-date survey.

There is nothing current in English to match it in rela-tion to the area it covers. In the past, Italian literature has been rather well served. The History of Italian Literature, by Francesco De Sanctis, came out in an English transla-tion in 1930 (reprinted 1959). First published in its origi-nal language in 1870–71, just when Italy was becoming a nation, De Sanctis' work was at first neglected because, as Benedetto Croce has told us, it reflected an earlier ro-mantic attitude hardly congenial to those constructing the new state. But readers after 1900 began to admire it and even formed a new school of criticism around it.

De Sanctis of course discussed Alessandro Manzoni, whom Mr. Pacifici begins with, but was too early to treat such authors as Giovanni Verga and Italo Svevo, who fig-ure so importantly at the end of Mr. Pacifici's book. To take another representative survey, there is Richard Gar-nett's A History of Italian Literature, written in 1898. That was the year of Svevo's second novel, Senilità (Senility), so Garnett can be excused for not knowing of it, and he may also be forgiven for overlooking the earlier volume, Un Vita (1892; A Life), since this was an obscure book written partly in Triestine dialogue by a businessman named Ettore Schmitz; and of course Svevo's masterpiece, La Coscienza di Zeno lay as far in the future as 1923. In any event, Garnett's book, good as much of it still is, has become outmoded in many aspects because of posterity's differing judgments; Garnett for example gives only a paragraph to Verga, and in the course of it does not mention even one of his works.

We are on more familiar ground with J. H. Whitfield's A Short History of Italian Literature, published in 1960. He takes up both Verga and Svevo, to Verga's advantage, and discusses many of the people who appear in Mr. Pacifici's study. But, like the books by De Sanctis and Garnett, Mr. Whitfield's deals with all aspects of literature and can therefore treat the novel only briefly; Mr. Pacifici can focus his entire attention on that genre.

He gives us first a 23-page "Background" chapter which interestingly prepares the way for his discussion of individual novelists. He shows above all why the Italians were not able to produce novels of any significance before the nineteenth century, and before Manzoni made his great breakthrough. He then takes us through Manzoni and seven other novelists, including the two mentioned earlier. Another of them, Antoni Fogazzaro, was once extremely popular in America, particularly for Il Santo (1905; The Saint). The thoroughness and expertness of Mr. Pacifici's investigation of all these writers make us all more eager to see the book he is now writing, a successor to the present one, which will bring the story up to date. He is making an important contribution not only to Italian studies but to a fuller understanding of world literature.

For these nineteenth-century Italian novelists do belong to world literature, and readers everywhere will find their works interesting and often valuable. Although Mr. Pacifici is modest in putting forth claims for them, many of them are rewarding to read. Manzoni's I promessi sposi (1825;

The Bethrothed) has long been regarded as an international heritage; in the early twentieth century it appeared in the Harvard Classics, and its current American edition in translation first appeared in 1956. Mr. Pacifici provides not only a useful examination of this historical novel, but a fine exposition of Manzoni's other work. He deals no less helpfully with various less-known novelists, then reaches his peak with Verga and Svevo. Although Gabriele D'Annunzio wrote much in the nineteenth century, Mr. Pacifici has saved him for the next book—another reason why we must anticipate that work. Meanwhile we have this first volume, and it is in itself a notable study of its subject.

HARRY T. MOORE

Southern Illinois University
May 30, 1967

CONTENTS

INTRODUCTION

IN THE PROLEGOMENA to my book, A *Guide to Contemporary Italian Literature* (1962) I remarked that one of the significant aspects of the postwar American rediscovery of Italian letters was an absorbing and fruitful interest in the poets and novelists of the past. My characterization of the phenomenon soon proved to be more accurate than I had hoped, and a number of translations and critical studies focusing on the Renaissance and the nineteenth century have afforded readers the opportunity of a more intimate glimpse of trends and artists of modern Italy.

My *Guide* was primarily concerned with explaining and analyzing the quality and meaning of a number of cultural manifestations in twentieth-century Italy—ranging from fiction and poetry to the cinema and the little magazines. Lack of space prevented me from doing more than offering a mere outline of the immediate background necessary to understand contemporary Italian writing. Indeed, in the course of writing my book, it had become increasingly clear to me that to comment extensively on the fathers of the contemporary novel in Italy and on the tradition they formed would inevitably mean writing one or more additional volumes that might serve as prologue and companions to my *Guide*.

It was this intention, coupled with the awareness that no single study in English dealing with the Italian novel is available to today's readers, that persuaded me of the necessity to prepare the present work. The last study of

the subject was written by the late Dr. Domenico Vittorini, and was published three and one-half decades ago.
Much has changed since then, as even a perfunctory
glance at the table of contents of his book would show.
Several of the novelists enjoying prominence in the late
twenties have sunk into oblivion, while others, chiefly
Nievo, De Roberto, and Svevo, have been subjected to
new evaluations that have enabled them to conquer a
more conspicuous position in their literature than the one
they formerly occupied. There is no need to be either
shocked or surprised by such sudden reversals of interpretations since we take for granted that, among all critical
activities, literary criticism is perhaps the most vulnerable,
for few of its judgments survive the changes of fashion
and taste. Nevertheless, the temptation of offering yet
another summing up is too strong to resist, all the more
since we assume that a greater historical perspective over
our material will permit us to consider our subject more
serenely and, hopefully, more sympathetically. And so we
must set ourselves to the task of rereading novels written
in an era which, in spite of its chronological nearness, was
vastly different from ours, and begin anew to measure
their scope, assess their achievement, define their vision,
and study their position in the context of an emerging
literary tradition.

The aims of what has been projected as a two-volume
study are simply to correct, modify, and otherwise extend
present knowledge of the Italian novel in English-speaking
countries; to try to answer, insofar as possible, certain
basc questions students inevitably ask in connection with
the novel in Italy: Who are the enduring novelists that
country has produced over the past century or so? In what
ways did they improve the native tradition of the genre?
In what specific manner can we read such works as reflections of the vast social, political, and economic changes
undergone by the nation? What insights into the human
predicament do they offer to the reader of today, and how
significant and relevant are such insights?

This book hardly claims to offer any final answers to

these and other questions. It does propose, however, to prepare the initiate to begin grappling with them, and, by providing him with a certain amount of factual information and interpretative comments, hopes to enable him to begin formulating independent, if tentative, judgments.

The scheme of this volume, and of the one that will eventually complement it, is simple. I have chosen a number of writers whose work seemed to be particularly apt to illustrate the development of the novel in modern Italy. Rather than attempting to study their entire literary production, I have generally limited myself to considering only the book or books that are most persuasively indicative of their vision as well as of the thematic, stylistic, and structural innovations they brought to the genre. Within the limitations of space, I have also touched briefly on those important biographical and literary events of my subjects when, by so doing, the meaning and significance of their work could be illuminated further. No detailed study of the selected number of writers included in this book has been attempted, and only three of them, for reasons which I trust my analyses will make clear, receive major treatment. The English titles of the works mentioned are given in parentheses after the Italian title. If the work has been published in an English translation, the place and year of publication precede the English title in the parentheses. The bibliographical section was composed to assist the reader who wishes to pursue the study of Italian fiction.

This book begins, as any dealing with the same subject invariably must, with Alessandro Manzoni and ends with the work of Italo Svevo. The choice was primarily dictated by chronological reasons, although Svevo, whose novels are rooted in naturalism, did not actually publish what many consider to be his most important book until 1923—almost three decades after his second novel. The projected sequel to this book will include a panoramic review of some significant nineteenth- and twentieth-century novelists, as well as discussions of Capuana, D'Annunzio, Pirandello, Deledda, Panzini, Tozzi, Bontempelli, Palazzeschi, Borgese, and other contemporary novelists.

I think it is only reasonable to state that this is neither a definitive nor an exhaustive account of my subject. There are omissions of both names and facts, and some may even challenge my selection, which has been at once personal and critical. With Luigi Russo, I believe that nineteenth-century fiction in Italy is not overly rich in great works. The novels I have chosen to discuss are the best and most typical of the genre the Italian sensibility and imagination were capable of creating.

It is my sincere hope that this volume will begin filling a regrettable lacuna in Italian studies, and that it will contribute to a firmer understanding of the novel. If it achieves its aim, the effort that went into writing it will prove to have been fully justified. I should feel doubly rewarded, however, if it will also stimulate others to re-study the relatively unexplored problem of the modern novel in Italy and offer other fresh interpretations of its quality and achievement.

The happiest pages for an author to write are those in which he records his expressions of gratitude to all those who, directly or indirectly, helped make his work possible.

I must begin by declaring a special debt to the John Simon Guggenheim Memorial Foundation for a Fellowship in 1961–62, which permitted me to begin work on this volume in Italy, in close proximity to the birthplaces and memories of the subjects of my study. A grant-in-aid from the American Philosophical Society enabled me to spend the better part of the summer of 1962 visiting additional libraries. A number of smaller grants from Yale University and the Olivetti-Underwood Corporation of America were used to defray expenses connected with a year of study and travel abroad and with the purchase of research material.

I should like to express my heartfelt thanks to at least some of my colleagues and friends for the interest with which they followed this book from its earliest draft to completion. I am grateful to all of them, but particularly to Henri M. Peyre, Rigo Mignani, Joseph G. Fucilla, Frank and Lillian Rosengarten, Paul Weiss, Martin Nozick, Robert W. Hartle, Jimmy and Dodo Hershman, and Professor Giuseppe Cardillo, Director of the Italian Cultural Institute in New York City.

This volume could not have been written without the cooperation and goodwill of the staff of Yale's Sterling Memorial Library, especially Messrs. Harry P. Harrison and Robert J. Olson. In Italy, I was once again fortunate to be able to count on the assistance of the staff of the Angelica and the Alessandrina Libraries. I am particularly obliged to Mr. Robert Connolly of the Paterno Library of Columbia University for his unfailing courtesy and cheerful hospitality.

Mrs. Florence G. Waldhetter and Mrs. Ellen Josepher of Queens College, my student assistant, Miss Marianne Pollini, and Mrs. Jackie Epstein typed the manuscript efficiently and competently.

Finally, my wife Jeanne must share the credit for whatever merit there is in this work. I thank her for keeping it alive when circumstances prevented my devoting full attention to it, for insisting that I keep my future audience in mind, and for reading and discussing with me every page of this book. I alone am responsible for whatever imperfections may still mar my exposition and interpretations.

My analyses are based upon a reading of the works in the original. In order to make the text easier to read, I have quoted from the standard English translations listed in each chapter. In all other cases, the translations are mine.

SERGIO PACIFICI

Larchmont, New York
January 12, 1967

The Modern Italian Novel

FROM MANZONI TO SVEVO

TO TELL A story—be it a tale of love, or one revolving around an adventure, an unusual or heroic confrontation, a strange encounter, or simply an amusing description of the tricks and deceits played by men on other men, thus making life the humorous and treacherous thing it is—has always held considerable fascination for mankind. History itself, through its deeds and documents, records how highly esteemed narrative art has always been in most countries the world over. In his influential and widely read treatise *Il cortegiano (The Courtier)* Baldassar Castiglione went as far as to list it among the essential attributes of a perfect gentleman.

"Story telling," writes Harry Levin in *The Gates of Horn*, "has always been, and will probably continue on being, one of the main continuities of culture; by that token it has been, and should continue to be, especially protean in its successive adaptations to cultural changes." Life goes on, never static or the same, and the changes it brings to society through developments of history, the growth of commerce, and human discoveries inevitably alter man's way of looking at himself and the world in which he lives. Such changes, often startling and dramatic, are ultimately reflected not only in the content but in the very expressive form through which each artist tries, however imperfectly, to seize, depict and illuminate a certain reality of the people, their customs and beliefs of his own age. Thus it was that in the Middle Ages the genre that best responded to the human imagination and interest was the epic poem, the *chanson de geste* of the Arthurian and Charlemagne cycles; later on, it was the short story (which survived its own period and has continued without interruption to our own day), skillfully practiced by such diverse artistic temperaments as Boccaccio and Chaucer. Still later, it was the romance of chivalry, which found in Ariosto, Tasso, and Spenser its best practitioners; finally, in modern times, it was the novel. Significantly enough, as Mr. Levin reminds us, "epic, romance and novel are the representatives of three successive estates and styles of life: military, courtly, and mercantile." The many radical changes undergone by society have made the novel the most popular mode of artistic expression. It is certainly no exaggeration to state that, since the eighteenth century, the novel has experienced nothing less than a meteoric ascendancy over all other literary forms, perhaps because it is so very accessible to the mass audience but also, I suspect, because a large body of writers has found it a versatile medium through which they can effectively dramatize man's dreams and aspirations, his fears and his hopes, his anguishes and joys in a journey toward self-knowledge and fulfillment.

Ever since the beginning of their literature, Italians have practiced the art of storytelling with considerable skill and consummate artistry. The annals of Italian letters are filled with the names of talented and frequently influential raconteurs who have brought special distinction and unusual vitality to the genre: the anonymous author of the thirteenth-century *Novellino*, Boccaccio, Sacchetti, Firenzuola, Bandello, the modern Capuana, Verga, Serao, Di Giacomo, and, in our century, Pirandello, Tozzi, Moravia, Buzzati, and Calvino are the first names that come to mind. Indeed, precisely because many students of literature have been aware of the existence of a rich narrative tradition in Italy, the question they regularly raise is: "If the *novella*, the courtly and heroic romances—genres in which Italy excelled—are the novel's most direct predecessors, why did Italy find herself in the retroguard with respect to the novel?" The question before us is, to be sure, so large and complex as to defy generalizations. But it might be answered, for the moment, by pointing out that like all creative manifestations the novel, too, is the product of certain countries that historically had reached a particular degree of social, political, and even economic emancipation. Speaking of three authors, almost universally acknowledged as the fathers of the modern novel—Defoe, Richardson, and Fielding—Ian Watt remarks in his perceptive study on *The Rise of the Novel* that "their geniuses could not have created the new form unless the conditions of the time had also been favourable." If the novel did not emerge in Italy until the early part of the nineteenth century—almost a century later than in England and France—we must assume that the social, political, and cultural conditions were simply unfavorable, or unreceptive, to the new genre.

Italian critics and literary historians are not very helpful here, since they have consistently chosen to ignore, or slight, a problem which should be considered most central in the development of their culture. A detailed discussion of the question of the novel in Italy—how it developed amidst intense polemics, how it grew patterning itself after the French example, and how it was eventually accepted by the public—could no doubt take us far indeed, as it would require a close examination of the history of Italy, the fabric of her culture and of her society from the beginning of the eighteenth century onward. Clearly any critic undertaking such a needed study must be well versed in several disciplines, ranging from literary history and criticism to sociology, and would be called upon to use a variety of approaches, from the statistical to the descriptive. Before arriving at a statement about his subject, he would have to take into consideration a whole spectrum of factors—economic, political, cultural, religious, and even psychological—to support his contentions. While we await such a study, and in order to place the problem at hand in its proper perspective, it might be useful to review briefly the chief circumstances that delayed the birth of the novel in Italy and the elements that determined its course throughout the better part of its first decades of life.

We may begin our inquiry by asking whether men of letters in Italy found it difficult, or even distasteful, to write novels. Was there something in their intellectual training or stance that prejudiced the chances of the new genre, perhaps because it was thought to be unworthy of an artist's efforts? The evidence at hand is scarce, but we may safely deduce that such must have been the case. Writing has always been, at least up to recent times, an activity proper to the literate; and in those days education was a privilege of the well-to-do, a class hardly interested in reaching a vast public and even less concerned with attempting to criticize, however indirect, the prevailing social order. In fact, "from 1845 onwards," as a recent observer of the Italian scene has written, "few had studied, or could have done so; in fact, everything that showed propensity toward free and independent studies focusing on the reasons and forms of art was vituperated. . . . In Sicily, in those times, there were no teachers, except the priests, whose culture did not go beyond the dead languages; as far as taste was concerned, they formed it on the translations of Church Fathers, Lent sermons and funeral orations." When the writer did not come from the affluent aristocracy or middle class, he was a professional in the contemporary meaning of the term, a person specifically hired by the nobility to instruct, amuse, or glorify the name of those who gave him sustenance. That even in such circumstances the writers often managed to preserve a modicum of artistic integrity, does them honor, to be sure. Nevertheless, it is easy to see how their special situation made it difficult, not to say improbable, to make genuinely critical statements on the world about them. Exceptions can always be found, of course. The eighteenth-century playwright Carlo Goldoni wrote several works in which he freely poked fun at the customs and manners of his day; and the sterner poet Giuseppe Parini displayed unusual boldness when he composed a longish poem, *Il giorno* (*The Day*), in which he painted a stinging picture of the purposelessness and decadence of the aristocratic *signori*. As a rule, however, Italian artists tended to avoid subjects that might prove to be controversial, and perhaps cause the loss of their enviable positions. One might observe that, by and large, a sort of conflict of interest developed—a conflict that could be resolved by turning the attention of the poet toward the self, or toward a past that by its very nature was nowhere as delicate a topic as the present. In a sense, then, it was the concept of literature as institution *sui generis*, and literature restrained or molded by practical affairs, that was detrimental to the rise of what proved to be a genre eager to focus on things as they were. Century after century saw the Italian artist invariably at the service of the ruling elite: Petrarch and Boccaccio held important posts, as did Dante in his day. The contrast could hardly be sharper, since only the latter writes with a moral indignation and a righteousness possible only to those who are excluded from the Establishment and must therefore write from the outside. Poliziano, Machiavelli, Ariosto, and Tasso, the chief writers of the Renaissance, were similarly employed, for varying periods of time, by the influential *mecenati* of their era; Parini himself was a preceptor with the Borromini and the Serbelloni families; Metastasio was the poet laureate at the court of Emperor Charles IV in Vienna. Others, Vittorio Alfieri, Ugo Foscolo, and Alessandro Manzoni among them, were more fortunate. Their independent means, or their unwillingness to become official mouthpieces of the ruling powers, enabled them to express what they thought or felt about the world with a degree of freedom unknown to, say, Vincenzo Monti. Generally, however, the writer in Italy accepted the condition of living in the uncommitted, secure, and exceedingly serene world of artistic creativity—a world in which the burning problems of the day lost their fire or urgency. In short, as Luigi Russo has acutely noted, the typical man of letters in Italy underwent a rigorous and essentially lyrical education, inaugurated by Humanism and the Renaissance.

Such an education, solidly grounded in the study of philosophy, theology, history, and the classics, placed a heavy emphasis, on the one hand, on the importance of literary traditions, and, on the other hand, on the supremacy of poetry over all the literary genres, since it was truly capable of reflecting the poet's personal dream. While most readily acknowledged that fiction could amuse, it was clear that it was hardly capable of pursuing the high and disinterested goals of poetry. Thus, in Russo's words, "the novel and the short story lay idle for a long time, and treatise writers and historians [alike] were hard put to hide their embarrassment toward such an inferior genre. Only during Romanticism and after the classical example of Manzoni, did the novel conquer its heraldry of nobility." But even when the novel was no longer looked upon with suspicion or contempt, there remained a vociferous nucleus of critics who persisted in arguing the case against the genre, upholding their contention that intellectually or temperamentally the Italians were ill-suited to cope with the requirements of a sustained type of narrative. The problem was that, while their assertions were often historically valid, they led the critics to make unjust statements or reach wrong conclusions as to why Italy seemed unable to produce good novels. Thus, the nineteenth-century poet Giacomo Leopardi, embittered by the intellectual corruption of his people and the frivolity of their culture, had observed: "The Italians themselves never think or write about their own habits, as if they thought that such studies were not important." And in a totally different vein, the twentieth-century polemicist Giovanni Papini, reviewing the state of the novel and appraising its achievements in its first century of life, came to similar conclusions about the basic flaw in the Italian imagination. For him, since the Italians seemed to lack the power of observation, introspection, and the ability to undertake moral analyses—the three qualities he found essential to novel-writing—they would do better to devote their creative energy to what he called a kind of "literature terribly serious, or at least instructive far more than amusing."

Neither observer had actually attempted to place the problem into perspective, and review the special circumstances that had made the development of the novel problematical in their country. A cursory examination of such circumstances is therefore essential to the understanding of the question before us.

It has frequently been remarked that among all literary forms the novel is perhaps the one that demands an unusually high degree of social stability. "The novelist," writes Martin Turnell, "like the dramatist has a clear conception of the nature of man, the world in which he lives, the principles to which he subscribes, the society to which he belongs, the rules which govern, or are supposed to govern, his conduct." "Society," notes J. S. Kennard, "must become self-conscious before it can be mirrored in a literary work." In a country politically fragmented, it was hardly possible to achieve the centralization of life which in other countries had materially contributed to strengthening the novel. It is not surprising to discover that, once Italy had achieved political unification, her culture experienced a sudden, and in many ways remarkable, flowering of novels. The political autonomy enjoyed by other nations had also been instrumental in changing the existing feudal order of society, and in stimulating the growth of a prosperous middle class that has long been regarded as one of the phenomenon that permitted and accompanied the ever-increasing popularity of a genre bent on criticizing, subtly or overtly, the *status quo*. The bourgeoisie, of whose life the novel soon became the best literary expression, was composed of merchants and tradesmen. Arnold Kettle in his *Introduction to the English Novel* states that "it was a revolutionary class. . . . The commercial bourgeoisie were revolutionaries against the feudal order because the feudal order denied them freedom. It denied them freedom, physically, legally, spiritually, to develop the way they must develop." The arrival on the scene of the middle class marks the beginning to an eventual collapse of a feudal society, and with it of a way of life, and human relationships which were incompatible with the new times. By the seventeenth century, for example, England had reached unorthodox positions that enabled people to view society not as the product of God but of men, and as such, subject to fundamental changes in its structure.

In most advanced nations in Europe, the middle class had also forced governments to work toward the improvement of schools, with a view to eradicating illiteracy. By contrast, the prevailing political situation in Italy actually stifled the emergence and emancipation of a liberal middle class, and the material and cultural advances it brought with it. Statistics speak impressively here: as late as 1862, the year of Italy's official unification, 78 per cent of its entire population, five years of age or older, was illiterate. Only by the end of the first decade of our century the great efforts of the various political cabinets had succeeded in producing a public school system which, however imperfect, was nevertheless capable of educating an ever-growing number of men and women who were to become the mass audience any novelist attempts to reach. With political autonomy, came also a new freedom, without which it is all but impossible to address oneself, however subtly or indirectly, to momentous questions. As Mr. Levin remarks, "the development of the novel runs parallel to the history of democracy and results in a gradual extension of the literary franchise." Anyone even superficially acquainted with modern history of Italy surely realizes the applicability of Mr. Levin's statement to the local situation. Indeed, the beginning of the novel in Italy coincides with, or was inspired by, the revolutionary movement and the subsequent wars of liberation (called Risorgimento) from which the country eventually emerged politically united. What were the conditions in Italy at the beginning of the nineteenth century, and just how did they affect the course and development of her literature? A quick glance at the political map of the country can be instructive to anyone attempting to find in history at least an influential force shaping artistic endeavors.

Ever since the sixth century, when the Lombards invaded Italy, and more systematically after the fall of the Swabian dynasty, the political structure of the nation had undergone a fragmentization that caused both the gradual disappearance of democratic institutions and the slow emergence of states ruled by tyrannical methods. Assassinations took the place of legal changes in the government; mercenary soldiers replaced the local army, and treachery, rather than justly and honestly administered treaties, became the rule of the day. Despotic rulers passed from the scene, only to be replaced by other rulers, at times benevolent but often even more ruthless than their predecessors. The states grew more and more jealous of each other, made alliances with non-Italian powers, and went so far as to develop a culture of their own. Their insularity at times fostered and reenforced a dialectal tradition that was to prove a formidable obstacle in the creation of a unified language and a national culture. Foreign powers, chiefly Spain and France at first, and later Austria, exploited the division of the country, and added more fuel to the flame of jealousy and hatred each state nourished for the other. Thanks to such division, they were able to make frequent predatory incursions into Italy and subjugate, for varying periods of time, a number of her regions. Foreign rule made its impact on the political as well as on the cultural plane. Some cities, in the North and South alike, managed at times to enjoy periods of cultural flowering even when governed by a foreigner, so long as he was sympathetically disposed toward artistic creativity and took pride in achievements of the spirit. Usually, however, the story was far from a happy one: in order to preserve and enhance his power, the despot simply had to sacrifice the well-being of the people. Indeed, only by keeping the masses in conditions of dismal ignorance, extreme poverty and always at their mercy, could the local feudal lords hope to preserve the established order.

In 1815, the situation was so dismal that it actually precluded any hope for the future. Thanks to the work of so-called statesmen, the clock had been turned back to the preceding century. Spain, Austria, and France continued to have a tight grasp on Italy's internal and foreign affairs, for the nation was a collection of states of varying size, governed by reactionary despots, or by people clearly opposed to the liberal winds that were blowing from England and, later on, from France herself. There were four main kingdoms and states: in the Northwest, the century-old Kingdom of Sardinia (comprised of Piedmont, Liguria, and Sardinia), ruled by Vittorio Emanuele I (soon to be succeeded first by Charles Felix and then by Charles Albert) of the branch of Savoy-Carignano; in the North and Northeast, the Kingdom of Lombardy-Venetia, ruled by the powerful Austrian Maria Theresa and Joseph II; in Central Italy, the Papal State, administered by Pius VII; in the South, the so-called Kingdom of the Two Sicilies (which included most of what today goes under the name of Mezzogiorno), ruled by Ferdinand I of the Bourbons. The balance of Italy was further split into yet smaller states: the Duchy of Modena, governed by Francesco IV of the Estensi family; the Grand Duchy of Tuscany, with Florence as its capital, ruled by Ferdinand III, of the Lorenesi family; the Duchy of Parma-Piacenza assigned to Marie Louise of Austria, wife of Napoleon, until her death after which it would return to the Bourbons. The work of Metternich, who had presided at the Congress of Vienna that had reshaped the order of Europe, has indeed produced a nation that was nothing if not a "geographical expression," untouched, except insofar as its intelligentsia was concerned, by the ideas of the Great Revolution or of the Enlightenment. Politically and economically, if not culturally, Italy was a backward country. As the historian René Albrecht-Carrié writes, "this backwardness . . . constituted a vicious circle, while a long period of subjection to foreign rule had served to dry up the springs of cultural life. During the seventeenth and eighteenth centuries, Italy had lost to others, to France in particular, the cultural leadership which had been hers during the flowering of the Renaissance. The active centers of life, political, economic, and cultural, had moved to the north, and it is essentially correct to say that despite notable exceptions and accomplishments, Italy was in the main a passive recipient of outside experiences."

The end of this dismal period of Italian history is marked by a series of revolutionary movements that led to the rebellions of 1820–21 and of 1831 in Naples (where the Constitution was first granted and later withdrawn), and intense underground activities, inspired and engineered by the so-called Carboneria. The Carbonari were courageous patriots, invariably intellectuals from the middle class and occasionally from the aristocracy, who were determined to organize rebellions anywhere where there was at least a chance that, by applying the necessary pressure, the constitution would be granted. The group collapsed after the revolt of 1831, and was replaced by a new political society called La Giovane Italia, the creation of an extremely serious and intelligent republican, Giuseppe Mazzini.

The political ferment of those years produced few tangible results, but it did create a climate of rededication to the ideals of freedom from tyranny and to the concept of national unity. It also gave rise to a literature with distinct patriotic overtones, best exemplified by the large body of writings of Mazzini himself (who, exiled from Italy, found refuge in England where he worked relentlessly to dramatize the plight of his country), Alessandro Manzoni, Silvio Pellico (whose memorable book *Le mie prigioni* was said to have cost Austria more than one lost battle), the poet Giuseppe Giusti, whose biting anti-Austrian epigrams captured the fancy and imagination of his readers. The two most distinguished and esteemed poets who unofficially participated in this group were Ugo Foscolo, himself a versatile critic and teacher, and, to a lesser extent, Giacomo Leopardi. Enlightened periodicals favoring political unification also came into being, among them *Gli Annali*, directed by G. D. Romagnosi, *Il Politecnico* and, later on, *La Rivista Europea*.

Even music found new vigor and meaning in the lives of all Italians, thanks to the operas of Rossini, whose *William Tell* was widely acclaimed, and the young Giuseppe Verdi, whose *Lombards of the First Crusade* struck a particular sensitive chord in the national pride of his fellow countrymen.

For the first time in their country's history, the efforts of the overwhelming majority of Italian artists—musicians, poets, novelists, and painters alike—were directed toward the single purpose of enhancing the concept of freedom by demanding justice and liberty for their nation, denouncing the tyranny of the Austrians and the Spaniards, and dramatizing the sufferings, persecutions, and humiliations endured by all those who placed their country's dignity above their personal well-being.

The appearance of what may well be called patriotic literature should not be attributed solely to the lofty idealism of a handful of intellectuals who believed steadfastly in their dream of a united Italy. A series of events had taken place before the beginning of the Risorgimento; their full significance was not to be understood until somewhat later. Inevitably, however, they served to expose Italy to the democratic ideals circulating in France and England, and prepared the ground for the rebirth of creativity in the arts that was to characterize much of the century. Mme de Staël's essay, "On the Manner and Usefulness of Translations" published in 1816 in the first issue of *La Biblioteca Italiana,* a Milanese review financed partly with Austrian money, is indicative of how literary discussions can frequently, if indirectly, sharpen the political consciousness of a nation. By discussing on the theoretical plane the necessity and art of translating great writers irrespective of their nationality, Mme de Staël called the attention of her public to what were the most irritating shortcomings of Italian culture. Her sharp remarks no doubt irritated many parochial minds; yet they did serve to underscore the necessity for Italy to enter the mainstream of European art. However hurt they felt, Italians were made aware of the provincialism of their interest, the timidity of their experimentations, and the necessity of a cultural expression that would reflect the multifarious changes the nation was experiencing during those years. In

the early part of the nineteenth century, this could ultimately mean only one thing: independence from all forms
of tyranny; freedom from the yokes that had checked all
impulses toward a free and open art, and freedom from
exploitation, censorship, and persecution. As a student of
the Romantic period, Miss Grazia Avitabile, writes

> A desire for independence, and even rebelliousness against
> established ways, a rising nationalism coexisting with an
> awareness of the brotherhood of man, restlessness, indi-
> vidualism, cult of heroism, introspection, a yearning for the
> infinite, for the mysterious, for the exotic, the importance
> of imagination and fantasy over that of reason and senti-
> mentalism—these are the main elements which obscurely
> and vaguely agitate the pre-romantic age and eventually led
> to romanticism.

In retrospect, it became clear that Romanticism itself,
which in Italy never reached the turbulent and polemical
character of French Romanticism, was not merely largely
synonymous to a large degree with the patriotic aspirations of the intelligentsia, but was the very force that
paved the way for the type of literature consonant with
the yearnings of the nation. Thanks to the work of a
genial mind, the novel became, almost overnight, the
most avidly read and discussed genre of modern Italy.

In the light of what has been said thus far, it is easy to
see why Manzoni's *The Betrothed* (published in 1827 and
substantially revised in 1840–42) should occupy such a
prominent place in the landscape of Italian letters. To
state that the novel is a milestone in the history of the
genre is, however, simply not enough. Its worth rests not
only in the international recognition it received, nor in the
fact that it is the first great novel written by an Italian in
modern times. Thanks to the originality of its form, the
boldness and geniality of the solutions it proposed to
vexing literary questions, the imagination of its content,
The Betrothed managed to do for fiction what Dante's
Comedy had succeeded in doing for poetry five and one-
half centuries earlier. The novel successfully presented an
absorbing synthesis of a complicated and wretched period

of Italian history and, at the same time, also offered some feasible solutions to thorny literary questions with which no writer before Manzoni had come to grips. Moreover, thanks to the example of its author, the novel gained substantial dignity and was transformed into an art form worthy of being practiced by the most talented minds. Up to Manzoni's time, in fact, writing a novel had generally not been thought of as being an altogether honorable undertaking. Carlo Varese, a respected and highly success-ful physician—as well as the clandestine author of several novels—confirmed his avocation only when his identity as a novelist was revealed and he was faced with the possible loss of reputation that threatened to destroy his profes-sional career.

Even when Manzoni, whose intellectual and patrician background was widely known, published his novel not everyone applauded the idea that such a fine poet should have lowered himself to the writing of fiction. One of his reviewers, writing for the authoritative magazine *La Bi-blioteca Italiana*, ironically remarked how "the news that the author of the *Adelchi*, the poet of the *Inni sacri* (*Sacred Hymns*) was writing a novel, had enobled the career [of fiction writing], and induced some fine minds to take it up," thus acknowledging, however reluctantly, the prestige the novel was rapidly acquiring.

The change in the prevailing climate to which I have briefly alluded was neither accidental, nor sudden, but a product of new needs and new visions. From the closing years of the eighteenth century there had been a tendency to acknowledge the "usefulness" of historical narratives as vehicles to explain the past and illuminate the present. The introduction in Italy of the novels of Sir Walter Scott—first in French translations and later in Italian—merely hastened what was an unreversable and irresistible trend that produced a cultural revolution of the first mag-nitude. An increasing number of writers began recognizing the possibility of exploiting the adventurous and dashing tales written in a Scottian manner to bring their case for political unification to the attention of the readers, if only under the guise of innocent historical stories. The chief problems remaining were to keep the reader's interest alive and to teach him to see in the tale the inescapable implications about the sorry state of his nation. The applause that greeted the publication of Manzoni's *The Betrothed* was indicative of the changed mood of a nation growing ever more restless and impatient with its political order. It became fashionable and almost *de rigueur* to write historical novels. Numerous writers, among them Grossi, Cantù, D'Azeglio, Nievo, Guerrazzi (whose first great novel was brought out in 1827, the year of *The Betrothed*), Rovani, followed in Manzoni's footsteps. Not until the nation had resolved the great issue of political unification was the novel to venture in new directions. To reach that point, however, it was imperative for the writer to resolve still another issue, the *questione della lingua*.

Dante Alighieri was not the first writer to use Italian, or the vulgate, the new language that had emerged mainly as the result of the corruption of Latin, after the year 1000 A.D. Prior to the beginning of the thirteenth century, the new language, spoken generally by the plebes, was used primarily as an instrument of oral communication. It was Dante who, after the earlier poetry of the Sicilian school of the court of Frederick II and the sophisticated philosophical compositions of Guido Cavalcanti, Guido Guinizelli, and others, produced the first sustained literary expression in Italian prose, *La vita nuova* (*The New Life*) and poetry, *The [Divine] Comedy*. The poets who were his contemporaries, or who came shortly after him—Petrarch, Boccaccio, and Poliziano—continued the tradition begun by the Florentine. They composed their work in either language, but to the end of their lives remained convinced—quite mistakenly as history was to prove—that it would be their work in Latin that would ultimately determine their position in the history of their culture.

After the disappearance of the masters of the *Quattrocento*, and beginning with the sixteenth century, the community of writers took up fairly rigid and well-defined positions vis-à-vis the problem of the literary language.

One group held that the works of Dante, Petrarch, and Boccaccio should serve as models to be scrupulously followed (in which case they became embroiled in long, petty, and frequently fruitless debates revolving around questions of morphology, pronunciation, and linguistic purity); another articulate nucleus completely rejected the use of Italian deeming the language incapable of the accessibility, precision, and scholarly range of Latin. The outcome was a disconcerting lack of agreement which resulted in acrimonious quarrels and antagonistic positions impossible to reconcile. The spread of Italian as a standard language, nationally spoken, understood, and written with a modicum of uniformity, was thus further delayed.

The political division to which the country was subjected for several centuries aggravated matters even more, since it placed an added advantage upon knowing French, Spanish, or German, not only because they were the languages of the ruling powers, but because frequently, as in the case of French, they were the tongues spoken by the international intelligentsia. The playwright Carlo Goldoni, for example, went so far as to compose some of his better plays and autobiography in French, so as to reach a wider public; while the Piedmontese poet Vittorio Alfieri, brought up to speak French, did not learn Italian until the age of eighteen, when he had his servant tie him to a chair until he had mastered the day's grammar lesson. Alessandro Manzoni wrote some of his most important theoretical papers in French and in 1827, after the publication of his novel, became so concerned with the flaws, irregularities and impurities of his own style, that he decided to spend several months in Florence, "to rinse [his] clothes in the Arno river," an expression by which he meant to convey his desire to reforge his style to conform with the living language as spoken in its birthplace. His undisciplined and imperfect knowledge of his native tongue, far from being a unique phenomenon, was a common occurrence, the result of the traditional training of an educated young man. Only when Manzoni prepared himself to reach an audience without a common language did he realize the difficulty, as Barbara Reynolds comments, of "using a language he [had] hardly spoken . . . and [was] therefore bereft of that communication between himself and his readers and the confidence of using an instrument equally intelligible to them both."

From the practical and political angle, the principle guiding Manzoni in his persistent attempts to resolve the vexing *questione della lingua* (to which he devoted almost half a lifetime) proved to be both sound and wise. That his views were not always original goes without saying, for the problem had been uppermost in the mind of other leading poets of the time. Ugo Foscolo, for example, in one of a series of discourses on the subject, had remarked how "in other European countries, educated people make use of the national language, and leave the dialects to the plebes. Now, in Italy, this is a privilege of only he who, traveling in nearby provinces, uses such a language that will permit him to be understood, and which may be called *mercantile* and *itinerant*. Whoever should scarcely depart from the dialect of the municipality, while living in it, would run the double risk of not being understood at all by the people and being derided because of his literary affectation." Manzoni, in a series of papers and through his own practice, came to the conclusion that a writer should use a spoken, and therefore living language, rather than the literary and frequently artificial idiom most artists had used since the Renaissance. It must have been due to his desire to be equally intelligible to all Italians that he unlearned the Milanese dialect and declared that all dialects should be sacrificed if Italy were to have a common language, both literary and spoken. The contemporary reader might easily accuse Manzoni of insensitivity to the values and possibilities of the dialects (both of which have amply been recognized and exploited in our day by such novelists as Carlo Emilio Gadda and Pier Paolo Pasolini). Nevertheless, it is difficult to deny that a national literature simply cannot exist without a national language, and that all linguistic experimentations must by necessity follow, not precede, its adoption. Indeed, Manzoni's decision to draw almost exclusively on the Tuscan as spoken in Florence may seem debatable today, since it led to inevitable excesses and errors. In its day, however, it was widely accepted as responsible and feasible, all the more since it managed to bring about a much needed and badly delayed linguistic unity that proved to be a turning point in the development of the novel in Italy. Only after Manzoni and the Unification, in 1861, did it become possible for a literary artist to write with the knowledge that he would be read and understood by his audience. By the same token, however, so narrowly was the Manzonian solution accepted that it soon became a convention unto itself, to be promulgated even at the cost of imitation, rather than to be improved. Only a few were bold enough to experiment with new ways of expression: some occasionally used regional dialects to bring an added note of vivacity and realism to the dialogue, among these were Fogazzaro and Tozzi; one, Giovanni Verga, actually fashioned a new language out of his native Sicilian dialect; and still another, Italo Svevo, for reasons having to do with his milieu and upbringing, wrote in a kind of Italian that could most felicitously be called, after Renato Poggioli, a *lingua franca*—a strange, and even awkward but supremely effective result of a kind of Italian written by a man who thought in German! The dichotomy literary language-dialect was pointedly underscored by one of Svevo's heroes (the protagonist of *The Confessions of Zeno*): "We lie with every word we speak in the Tuscan tongue! If only he [his psychiatrist] knew how we tend to talk about things for which we have the words all ready, and how we avoid subjects which would oblige us to look up words in the dictionary! That is the principle which guided me when it came to putting down certain episodes in my life. Naturally it would take on quite a different aspect if I told it in our own dialect." In the intriguing story of the language problem in modern Italian letters, both Verga and Svevo rank as exceptional figures. The novel in Italy has always experienced its share of modest, if valuable, innovations on the structural level. By and large however, its practitioners have consistently preferred working with a language patterned on Manzoni's masterpiece. Discounting the stylistic novelties present in many a major or minor work of fiction, it is safe to say that only recently has the Italian novelist truly attempted to find a new language, consonant with his vision of a violent, dehumanized, and anxious civilization.

The completion of the groundwork necessary for a much-sought linguistic unity was accompanied by other pivotal developments. For one thing, once independence was achieved, cultural exchanges became freer, more regular and productive. While Italy had been under foreign domination it had been hazardous, and at times even impossible, to read foreign authors whose views were not consonant with those of the established order. In the newly declared Kingdom of Italy, a free intellectual intercourse, based on dialogue, information, and evaluation, became possible at last. Journalists and novelists alike immersed themselves in the reality of their time, enjoying their hard-won freedom to travel, speak, and write about what they saw and felt without fear of recrimination or persecution. Whereas it had formerly been unfeasible or even dangerous to write frankly and accurately about the various ills plaguing the less fortunate regions of the North and South alike, it became a matter of personal commitment to investigate, analyze, and report on the sufferings endured by millions of people, living in a most abject state of poverty and ignorance, waiting for help to arrive from the seats of power, the cities.

Italian writers wishing to achieve such a goal did not have to search far, and much less invent, the technique needed to transport the condition of their era into art. Since its earliest times, there had always been a strong tradition of realism in their literature. Now, they proceeded to combine the realistic vein with the idealism of Romanticism which had taught them how literature can frequently be synonymous with a human yearning to be a free agent in a world of fear. Romanticism had stressed the personal and the subjective; realism, known in Italy as *verismo*—true to reality, or close to truth—prodded them to insert a condition of sorrow and deprivation into the context of a personal but also universal condition.

Immediately before and after Manzoni the novel had distinguished itself by its sustained interest in the historical events that had made possible Italy's political independence. Nievo, Rovani, De Roberto, and Fogazzaro recounted the agonies and adventures of young patriots, or would-be patriots, how they worked to bring about freedom for their country, or how they had willfully proceeded to betray the ideals of the revolutionary movements and of the Risorgimento. The fiction of the *veristi*, influenced to a considerable extent by the realistic and naturalistic trends in France, strove to present a tale that would let life speak for itself, without sermonizing or proselytizing, hoping that the emerging picture would induce the reader to want to change a shameful condition. "Romanticism," writes Giulio Marzot, "had striven to reach the heart of reality and had prodded the reader through the medium of feeling. Sentiment could bring about an awareness and improvement of the spirit and, in turn, of social life. Realism, on the other hand, tended to discover the law for each phenomenon, and illuminate the reason which (once it had been made more experienced of all organs and levers of the physiological and psychological mechanism by acting on the mechanics of nature) would bring about the elimination of vice and of errors in the world. Through science, [realism] could [also] determine the progress and perfectionment of the individual and of the [human] species, in the context of a more evolved and admirable society."

Inevitably, then, historical circumstances influenced the course of the novel to a degree perhaps then unsuspected by most artists. The history, folklore, and life of Italy's colorful regions became the stuff of fiction, through which a statement about the local and the universal situation was articulated. Milan and the Veneto region, the Tuscan Maremma, Naples, Calabria, and the barren towns of Sicily, became the new settings of realistic literature. Depicted with painstaking accuracy as the locales of such novels were, they were transformed into timeless symbols of places where a hard-working, basically hopeless, frequently engrossing share of mankind lived in sin and despair, obsessed with the needs of their bodies far more than with those of their spirit. Following and intensifying the example of Manzoni, and as Archibald Colquhoun reminds us, "*Verismo* concentrated on the 'unknown millions whom history ignored,' as Manzoni had called them: the labourers, petty farmers, artisans, whose hopes had been aroused and dashed." But, unlike Manzoni's heroes, the characters of the novels written in the last decades of the nineteenth century believed that salvation *hic et nunc* and the achievement of a measure of fulfillment were the most elementary goals toward which man should strive in his quest for earthly happiness. The writer's awareness of important, and theretofore slighted social conditions brought him to reconsider the validity of certain literary techniques that had prevailed until then, and subject them to inevitable changes more in tune with what they strove to depict. "Realism itself," Harry Levin notes, "is itself a historical development: it registers the impact of social changes upon artistic institutions, brings about the breakdown of old conventions and the emergence of new techniques, and accelerates the momentum of the novel toward an increasing scope and flexibility." If it is possible to generalize again at this point, it is fair to state that the chief technical innovation brought about by the *veristi*, as exemplified in the work of its leading exponent Giovanni Verga, took the form of an objectivity that seemed to border on a total impassivity on the part of the author toward the creations of his imagination. Two other features singled out *verismo* from previous movements: a naïve confidence that the scientific method, if properly applied, would enable the novelist to resolve some of the fundamental questions about the lot of the human kind; and a concentrated effort to eliminate from fiction as legitimate focus of consideration many of the elements that prevented the artist from formulating a comprehensive statement about man—simply because such elements could not be measured, counted, appraised. The emphasis was put on the probable, not on the unusual; on the real, not on the imaginary; on facts, not on speculations. There is more than the usual ounce of truth to Gide's observation that 'the realists begin with facts and accommodate their ideas to facts." Verga's *roba*—the property of which everyone suddenly became conscious in an increasingly more affluent middle class—triumphed in fiction, though not to an extent comparable to that of the French novel. Human passions were described and analyzed in all their lusty, erotic manifestations, while patriotic feelings, noble idealism, genteel aspirations and romantic love which had permeated most of the early Italian novels, suddenly vanished from the scene. The reader then found himself confronting a tale concerned with describing the nature and effects of man's folly, man buffeted by the passion of his flesh and by his greedy attachment to things. "After proclaiming themselves the apostles of a new science," complains J. S. Kennard with some justification, "the pioneers of a new art . . . circumscribed the range of their studies to the sexual appetite, which they insisted is the instinct which controls humanity. The anatomy of man's body and soul was reduced to a single function; the endless variety of human tempers was summed up as diversity of temperament. . . . The method was bad; yet, by enlarging a novelist's field of action, it prepared for the transformation of the realistic into the psychological novel."

Actually, the third turning point in the history of the novel in modern Italy was brought about by a complex combination of a number of factors. Once unification of the country had been achieved, and interest in exploring life in its region partly exhausted, writers, again under the influence of the French example, grew increasingly more fascinated by the psychological motivation of human actions. While some of the early practitioners of what some call the psychological novel were *veristi*, as, for example, Luigi Capuana, the theoretical high priest of the trend, and De Roberto, the genre cannot be said to have found its best exponent until Italo Svevo. Considering the traditional lack of interest in human psychology then distinguishing the Italian temperament, it is not surprising that the Triestine novelist should remain largely ignored until a few years before his death in 1928. The tradition of a novel more concerned with the workings of the human psyche than man's drama and social ills, was given impetus thanks to the unorthodox narratives of Luigi Pirandello (who soon after the turn of the century abandoned the novel and the *novella* for the theater), Federigo Tozzi, and, a little later, Alberto Moravia.

At the beginning of the century much had changed on the cultural scene: the middle class had grown substantially, the nation enjoyed a higher standard of living, the nation was well on her way toward linguistic unity. These, and other reasons—the spread of literacy, the availability of books in popular editions, priced within the means of most working people—had finally created a climate in which the novel could thrive, certain that there was a public eager to read it (if not in book form certainly in serial form), conscious of its possibilities, of its capacity both to reflect upon, and interpret a historical period. Several additional years were to pass, however, before the Italian audience, conditioned—whether out of snobbishness or lack of perspective is a moot point—to favor the worst manifestations of writing so long as they were imported, learned to understand and appreciate the talented work of its native tradition. But that, as a famous novelist once wrote, is another story.

2 ALESSANDRO MANZONI: THE HISTORICAL NOVEL

ASK ANY EDUCATED Italian to name the two greatest literary artists his nation has produced, and his answer will invariably be Dante and Manzoni. Read and revered in every Italian school and home, avidly commented upon, discussed, and explained, Manzoni has few rivals in his country in terms of reputation and popular appeal. Indeed, with the exception of the *Comedy*, no other book has been the object of more intense scrutiny or more sustained scholarship than *I promessi sposi* (New York, 1956; *The Betrothed*), many of whose lines, along with the *Comedy*'s, have become part and parcel of the rich storehouse of popular proverbs and of the spoken language. The editions of the novel are said to number over five hundred, and a translation of it exists in most modern languages. The monographs, essays, notes, and minutiae on every conceivable aspect of Manzoni's life, ideas, and literary output run to the thousands—enough to fill the crowded shelves of the Casa del Manzoni in Milan which serves as the Center of International Studies on the writer.

The imposing and evergrowing Manzoniana has compounded the difficulty of adding something original to the exhaustive studies of his main biographers and critics, De Sanctis, Croce, Galletti, Momigliano, Barbi, Ghisalberti, De Robertis, and Colquhoun among others. Nevertheless, so central is Manzoni's position in the history of the modern novel in Italy, so extensively has he affected the course of her literature from the Risorgimento to our

post-World War II years, and so profoundly has he influenced, to one extent or another, the writers who followed him, that any discussion of the art of the novel in
Italy must inevitably begin with a consideration of *The
Betrothed*. Moreover, any foreigner wishing to understand modern Italy, her culture, people, and temperament
finds Manzoni as indispensable as Balzac, Flaubert, and
Baudelaire are necessary to understand the spirit of modern France, or Whitman, Hemingway, and Faulkner to
grasp at least the essence of America, and Scott, Dickens,
and Jane Austen to perceive the qualities of British culture. "*I promessi sposi*," as A. Passerin d'Èntreves felicitously noted some years ago, "is one of those books which,
together with the *Divine Comedy*, accompany the life of
the great majority of Italians . . . from the cradle to the
grave." "In more than one way," adds Richard Chase in
his essay on Manzoni in the European context, "the lives
Manzoni has created are 'archetypes' of Italian society."

In every respect, Manzoni is, along with the poet Giacomo Leopardi, a seminal figure in the history of his
literature. In the words of Leonardo Olschki, he represents
"the polarity of the Italian spiritual heritage and of contemporary European trends of thought and action," for it
is one of the implications of his novel that "no social and
political renewal of mankind and of [his] country was
possible without a revival of the moral conscience." By
virtue of his only and unique novel, Manzoni established
himself as the artist that simultaneously gave his country a
prose style that was to serve as model and inspiration for
future generations of writers and a work of fiction that,
thanks to the exceedingly favorable reception it received
in intellectual circles everywhere, actually paved the way
for a general acceptance in Italy of a new and theretofore
disparaged genre.

Manzoni's importance, nevertheless, is not exclusively
determined by his *Betrothed*. The body of his writings—
consisting of a handful of lyrical compositions, two tragedies in verse, a historical study, a religious treatise and a
wealth of miscellaneous papers—has always attracted the

attention of the critics. And justly so, for his numerous pronouncements on poetry, on the novel, drama, Romanticism, Catholic morals, his original *prise de position* vis-à-vis the irksome *questione della lingua*, are marked by originality, if not always genius, and by a profound intelligence. Moreover, they frequently serve to illustrate the period in which he lived as well as the critical stances that were to play a decisive role in shaping the product of his creative imagination. That from the critical point of view Manzoni was not always consistent, is of little or no consequence. What matters is that he remained always a mind eager to explore, study, reevaluate the large questions close to his creative interest and that, thanks to such a spirit, he was capable of achieving considerable detachment toward his work. Placing Manzoni in perspective and determining his position in the history of the modern Italian novel necessitates at least a glimpse of his main critical postures and of some of the ideas he expressed about the literary genres toward which he gravitated.

The man who would eventually be acclaimed the father of the novel in Italy, was born in Milan, on March 7, 1785, of an aristocratic and affluent family. His mother was Donna Giulia, the daughter of Cesare Beccaria, an eminent criminologist and the author of the treatise *Of Crimes and Punishment*. His presumed father was Don Pietro Manzoni, a conservative, minor Lombard aristocrat whose chief preoccupation seems to have been the management of his estate. Their marriage was far from happy; and in order to spare the youngster the pain of being a witness to their frequent quarrels, they decided to send him off to a boarding school, administered and staffed by a religious order. The experience there proved to be wretched, and certainly contributed to Manzoni's youthful disdain toward the organized Church and its politics. When he was seven, his mother arranged for a legal separation from her husband. She then left Milan, and settled in Paris where she lived for a number of years as the mistress of Carlo Imbonati, a Milanese banker, patriot, and esteemed gentleman who died in 1805.

By 1801, Manzoni had finished his formal school training. He returned to Lecco, near Milan, and to his father's home, where, with the encouragement of his aunt, he devoted himself to furthering his education. He immersed himself in reading, became a regular auditor of university lectures, and struck up a friendship with a vast number of prominent intellectuals and writers, among whom were Ugo Foscolo, Vincenzo Monti, the revolutionaries Giambattista Pagani, Ermes Visconti, Federico Confalonieri, as well as the historians Vincenzo Cuoco, Francesco Lomonaco, and Carlo Botta.

After the death of Imbonati, in whose honor he composed an extraordinarily moving poem, Manzoni joined his mother and took up residence in Paris. He lived there intermittently for several years, thereby having the enviable opportunity of becoming well acquainted with a culture and a nation he esteemed above his own. Donna Giulia's prime concern was now to find an acceptable match for her son. By 1807 (after Alessandro had been summoned hastily to Lecco by his dying father), she found a lovely sixteen-year-old girl by the name of Henriette Blondel, daughter of a prominent family of Swiss merchants and bankers, an eminently suitable bride for her son. Arrangements for their marriage were made and, in spite of inevitable complications stemming principally from the fact that the Blondels were not Catholic but Calvinists, the wedding took place on February 6, 1808.

What has long been regarded as the most central incident in Manzoni's life took place sometime after his marriage to Henriette. The event was to change the entire course of his private existence and give a new direction to his art. In his youth, Alessandro had been markedly critical of the Church, disparaging its political stances and its reactionary lack of sympathy for the patriotic aspirations of liberal Italians. In the light of prolonged interviews and conversations he held with the Abbé Eustachio Dègola and, in a second phase, with Monsignor Tosi (who had become his spiritual father), Manzoni began reexamining his beliefs and stands on matters of religion. There is still considerable disagreement among Manzoni scholars as to whether Henriette's decision to accept the spiritual guidance of the Abbé was not ultimately responsible for Manzoni's reevaluation of his own agnosticism. It is likely that Alessandro found the political ideas of the liberal Abbé quite attractive, especially since they tended to erase from his memory those conservative views of the Church that had repelled him in his younger days. However this may be, what is certain is that shortly after the birth of the couple's first child Giulia, in December, 1808, Manzoni formally requested the Vatican's permission to have his marriage ceremony repeated according to the Catholic rite—a request that was granted some time later, thereby permitting the couple to have their wish fulfilled on February 15, 1810.

The occurrence that has repeatedly been mentioned as having completed Manzoni's return to his Church is perhaps the most perplexing of his biography. Shortly after a two-month honeymoon at their Brusaglio estate, Henriette and Alessandro returned to Paris. There, on April 2, 1810, while watching the festivities organized to celebrate the marriage of Napoleon and Marie Louise, the misfiring of a rocket caused momentary panic among the spectators. Manzoni lost sight of his wife, and for several moments thought that she had been killed, crushed by the people running away in fear. He managed to find refuge in a nearby Church, where he prayed to God, and asked that his wife be restored to him. Suddenly, as the story has it, he felt tranquil and sure that his prayers would be heard by the Lord. He returned to his apartment in Place Vendôme, and found his wife safe and sound, waiting for him.

After their conversion, the couple moved back to Milan, where they were to live uninterruptedly for many years. The spiritual tranquillity attained after their crisis and the comfortable economic situation they enjoyed permitted Manzoni to lead a life without worries, dedicating himself to writing and to his favorite hobby of gardening and horticulture. He also spent some time supervising the affairs of his estate—happily, he found his activities conducive to the meditation and peace he needed for his literary work.

He began his literary career around 1812. By 1815 he had completed four of his projected *Inni sacri* (*Sacred Hymns*). He also finished two tragedies in verse, *Il conte di Carmagnola* and *Adelchi*, set respectively in the fifth and eighth centuries; both plays represent the author's official break with the neoclassical poetics of the three unities. In 1821, upon receiving word of the death of Napoleon, he composed one of his most celebrated and impressive lyrics, *Il cinque maggio* (*May 5*) (London, 1904; *Napoleonic Ode* [*of Manzoni*]), a moving tribute to the genius and universality of its hero. During the same year he began working on *The Betrothed*, the novel that was to demand most of his creative time throughout the following two decades. Aside from philosophical, historical, linguistic, and religious papers, Manzoni produced very little poetry after the completion of his masterwork.

The years between 1833 and 1873 brought him a mixture of public recognition and private grief. The success enjoyed by his book in both of its versions was certainly insufficient to make up for the numerous personal losses he had to sustain: in 1833, his wife, Henriette, died; his mother passed away in 1841, and twenty years later he lost his second wife, Teresa. Before he was to reach the end of a rich, rewarding but, in the main, uneventful existence, he was to see six of his eight children die. Some years after Italy had achieved unification, Manzoni was named senator, in recognition of his stature as a writer and of the contribution he had made to the cause of political unification. He died on May 22, 1873, in his Milanese house in Via Morone.

Everything Manzoni ever wrote—letters, critical essays and poems—was always subjected to numerous drafts and inevitable revisions and corrections. Usually nothing left his desk until he was completely satisfied with the manner in which the content had been expressed. None of his writing, however, occupied so large a part of his life as the book that was to make him immortal. It is not an exaggeration to say that Italian literature knows of few other works that had as fascinating a history as that of *The Betrothed.*

The novel was begun in 1821, and provisionally titled "Fermo e Lucia." By the time it had reached the printer's shop, the title itself was changed, first to "Gli sposi promessi," then to *I promessi sposi,* and the entire work had undergone several revisions. No sooner was the book published, than Manzoni set himself to reshaping it, and to preparing the final version which appeared in 1840–42. In all, he worked two decades on a tale that remains, to this date, a true model of purity of style and lucidity of vision.

During the composition of the novel, he kept his friends informed of the progress he was making, and discussed with them some of the problems of style and content he was encountering. Such letters (still uncollected in a systematic and scholarly manner) are particularly fascinating and significant in that they throw much light on his creative process and poetics. Thus, for example, in a letter written to M. Fauriel on May 29, 1822, Manzoni announced his novel in these words

> I scarcely dare add yet another few words on a literary project. . . . You must know that I am immersed in my novel, the subject of which is placed in Lombardy, between 1628 and 1631.
>
> The memoirs that have come down to us from that period give a picture of a very extraordinary state of society: the most arbitrary government, combined with feudal and popular anarchy; legislation that is astounding, both in its claims and its results; a profound, ferocious, pretentious ignorance; classes with opposite interests and maxims; some well-known anecdotes preserved in trustworthy documents, which develop all this very much; finally, a plague that gives

reign to the most consummate and shameless excesses, to the most absurd prejudices, and to the most touching virtues, etc. etc. . . . That's the stuff to fill a canvas, or rather that's the stuff that may only show up the incapacity of the person who sets to work on it.

The work planned was to take the space of a historical novel, patterned to some extent after the work of Sir Walter Scott whom Manzoni admired and whose fiction was enjoying a brilliant vogue at the time in Italy. In the same letter to M. Fauriel, Manzoni offered further thoughts on the genre.

To show you briefly what my chief idea about historical novels is, I will tell you that I conceive them as representing a state of society by means of action and characters *so similar to reality that they could be believed to be true history which has been just discovered.* When historical events and characters are mingled with this I think they should be represented in the most historical manner. (Italics mine).

The first draft of the manuscript was finally completed on September 17, 1823. From then until 1826, Manzoni dedicated himself to the task of revising and correcting his work. Several annoying delays and an unusually long production at the printers prevented the book from appearing until June 15–17, 1827. But the immediate and enthusiastic reception accorded to *The Betrothed* compensated the author for the immense labor and worrying he had poured into his novel during its prolonged gestation. Over six hundred copies of the book were sold in the first twenty days after its publication, much to the surprise and delight of the entire Manzoni household. Nine editions were readied and sold out before the year was over—a veritable record indeed considering the times, the high incidence of illiteracy in Italy, and the exorbitant price of the book. Yet Manzoni, pleased and gratified as he was with the fate of his book, was far from being completely happy with the results of his labor. Although the novel had been thoroughly corrected and revised before being committed to print, Manzoni set himself to work on it again, with an eye to improving not only the flow and harmony of the story itself, but its very style. Only then, he must have felt, would *The Betrothed* achieve that ideal tone of style and balance of themes any literary masterpiece should possess. The long and busy years during which he literally rewrote his book, from beginning to end, were to bear their fruit. Moreover, the definitive edition—upon which all critics' estimates are based—proved to be genuinely superior to the first edition. Second versions of a masterpiece, as Bernard Wall justly reminds us, "are often inferior to first versions," as Tasso's reworking of *La Gerusalemme liberata* clearly attests. The definitive version of *The Betrothed* allows us to follow "the improvements of Manzoni's craftsmanship . . . [It] was very much more muted than his earliest," for there "he preferred to suggest rather than narrate, and he left more to the readers' imagination. He was a master of the 'work of the file' in the classical or Virgilian sense."

What is *The Betrothed* about? On the surface at least, the question is easily answered, for the novel's plot is possibly one of the most conventional in the history of Western fiction. The German Italianist Karl Vossler once compared the book to a fairytale, since the story has a happy ending and the young man does indeed get his girl at the end of their adventures. Briefly stated, the book revolves around the love of two young silkweavers, Renzo Tramaglino and Lucia Mondella. Their marriage plans are spoiled by a ruthless local bully, Don Rodrigo. Viewed from this angle, the tale has a deceptive simplicity, and exhibits many of the qualities of the romantic, and colorful novels in the Scottian tradition. Nothing could be further from the truth. Not only is Manzoni a writer infinitely more complex than Scott, but he strives to go well beyond a mere blending of facts and fancy. The manifold adventures the two young lovers experience before their goal can be achieved, the long period of trials and tribulations that test their strength, courage, and dimension as human beings are never visualized, and even less described, as fascinating events per se. They are, rather, presented as parts of an intricate design, a pattern ordered by a Supreme Being who governs the universe. Through the events that form the spine of the book, and through the dialogues, monologues, and descriptions that are the very fabric of the novel, the author meant to illustrate the presence of Divine Justice on earth, a Justice that triumphs even when men, overcome by their miseries or about to lose their faith, wonder whether their Father has forsaken them, abandoning them to the forces of evil. The function of each episode in the book not only serves to keep the reader interested in the fictional fate of its heroes, but enables him to extract a lesson, a moral lesson in the highest sense of the term, bound to implicate the reader himself—leading him to a more thorough understanding of the meaning of the human condition.

Viewed from still another angle, it might be said that the vitality of the book is not so much in its ordinary sequel of events that leads us to an inevitably happy resolution of the central crisis, but in the fact that the incidents themselves are skillfully used to paint an absorbing tableau of the events, customs, and manners of a nation during a certain crucial period of its history. Through the book, we see the meaning of a political fragmentation resulting from centuries of internecine wars, petty jealousies, and dependence on foreign intervention or domination to solve internal national affairs. Thus the book becomes an accurate mirror of historical conditions existing long before the wars of the Risorgimento, as well as a telling commentary on the contemporary historical scene. Manzoni's range is so broad, and so acute is his political insight—disagree as we may with his diagnosis of the true reasons for the existence of evil in the world—that precious little escapes his attention, certainly nothing that would add to the interest of the tale he is narrating. A great historical tragedy unfolds before our eyes: a local government literally unable to come to grips with the problems confronting its subjects; a moral degradation that has rendered the ruling class incapable of leading the people or inspiring their confidence; a Church frequently corrupt, or guilty of debasing practices, manipulated by external pressures and torn by internal political schisms; and, last but not least, a vast cast of *popolani* displaying their historical stupidity, often equally incapable of listening to the counsels of reason or the instincts of the heart.

One might argue that in ordinary circumstances the two youths would hardly have had to go through so many hardships just to get married. But the years in which their tale is set, 1628–31, were far from being normal in any sense of the term. In a letter Manzoni wrote to his friend, M. Fauriel, in the summer of 1823, he claimed that he was attempting "to paint sincerely the period and country in which I have placed my story. The materials are rich; everything that shows up the seamy side of man is there in abundance. Assurance in ignorance, pretension in folly, effrontery in corruption are, alas, among many others of the same kind, the most salient characteristics of the period. Happily, there are also men and traits which honour the human race; characters gifted with a strong virtue, remarkable by their attitude to obstacles and difficulties, and by their resistance, and sometimes subservience, to conventional ideas." The pressure and threats of the local tyrant succeed immediately in achieving their goal; for the small town parish priest who is supposed to perform the wedding, Don Abbondio, out of fear for personal safety is easily persuaded to slight his duty. Only by avoiding a direct confrontation with Don Rodrigo's *bravoes* can the priest, hardly a "man born with the heart of a lion," navigate the stormy waters ahead. The wedding is put off with technical, religious reasons Renzo (who does not speak Latin) fails to comprehend. Intuitively persuaded that the priest is acting on orders from above, and subsequently informed by Don Abbondio's servant Perpetua that such is indeed the case, Renzo, on the advice of Lucia's mother, Agnese, takes his case to doctor Azzeccagarbugli (Quibble-Weaver), a well-known lawyer. Through a strange and highly amusing misunderstanding, the lawyer takes Renzo for a *bravo* seeking protection from the law. When Renzo shouts the truth, Quibble-Weaver, himself an admirer and protégé of Don Rodrigo, throws him out in a rage. Now it is the turn of Fra Cristoforo, a wise and honest friar who has befriended the couple, to be summoned for advice. The friar decides to take the matter up directly with the cause of all the trouble, but his attempt is of no avail. At the castle of Don Rodrigo, however, he discovers that the arrogant *signorotto* is planning to kidnap Lucia. Agnese's own plan to have the marriage officially recognized by having the two declare, before two witnesses, that they are man and wife also fails, for the priest goes into a short, but effective, fit and flees. Having exhausted all possibilities, the three decide to part: Renzo goes to Milan, in search of work, while the two women depart for a convent in nearby Monza, where they are placed under the protection of Benedictine nuns.

Calamities follow other calamities. Renzo arrives in Milan during the bread riots and is arrested as an *agent provocateur*. Fortunately, as he is taken to jail, he succeeds in arousing the sympathy of a crowd terribly hostile toward the government, and manages to escape. Lucia, who thought she would be safe in the convent, is betrayed by the very nun who was supposedly protecting her. She is kidnapped by the *bravoes* of another powerful criminal, to whom Don Rodrigo has appealed for help in carrying out his plan. Fortunately, through a miraculous intervention of Divine Providence, Unnamed (*Innominato* being the word Manzoni uses in this case, following the Anonymous Chronicler who is supposedly the original author of the story) repents for a life of crimes, and is converted by Cardinal Federigo Borromeo who is visiting the town. Lucia and her mother are placed under the protection of a family of decent, if misguided, people—Donna Prassede and Don Ferrante. Renzo, informed at last that Lucia is alive, leaves once again for Milan, hoping to find her. This time the city is in the grip of a devastating plague, and Renzo himself is mistaken for one of the *untori* (anointers—people suspected of having spread the deadly virus of the plague) and barely escapes the wrath of the crowd. He finally reaches the *lazzaretto*, the refuge place of all those struck by the plague, and there he falls in with Fra Cristoforo who is spending his last months on earth assisting the sick. In the *lazzaretto* he also finds Lucia who has recovered from the plague and is waiting to return to the village. It is in the *lazzaretto* that we see, for the last time, Fra Cristoforo, who releases Lucia from a vow of virginity made when she was in a cell in the castle of the Unnamed. Now that Don Rodrigo and his not-so-faithful henchman Griso have died, together with many wicked and good people alike, the three can return to their abandoned home by the lake of Lecco. No longer threatened by Don Rodrigo, Don Abbondio can peacefully perform a much-postponed wedding ceremony; and the two lovers settle in a small town near Bergamo, where they have their first child, a girl, whom they promptly name Maria.

Neither a summary of the book, however complete (and mine has merely tried to give the main outline of its plot), nor the author's own attempts to define his aim, succeed in giving an accurate idea of the complexity and extraordinary beauty of *The Betrothed*. "Perhaps," as Mr. Colquhoun has noted, "it is the unfolding impression of hidden layers of meaning that contribute so much to the fascinating humanity of the book." However one reads it, *The Betrothed* is always an absorbing story about people, their simple aspirations and complex greed, their hopes and their frustrations, the power they yield, and the despicable desires that drive them—but also people who are caught in the mysterious workings of history. Not the least remarkable feat of the book is that it shows us the drama of two peasants who are the focal point of the novel simply because, for inexplicable reasons, they become at once makers and protagonists of that immensely fascinating drama we call history.

As a matter of fact, the prominent role historical events play in the novel is the element that has consistently, and inevitably, led to the facile and erroneous categorization

of *The Betrothed* as a historical novel. The label, undoubtedly useful for general purposes, is bound to generate some misunderstanding about the nature of Manzoni's
work, unless the author's special concept of the genre is
taken into account. Indeed, particularly to the student of
English literature, the term itself recalls to mind the works
of Sir Walter Scott, who, when told that the Italians owed
everything to him, is reported to have exclaimed, "In that
case [*The Betrothed*] is my best work!" In Manzoni's
novel one finds neither the glorification of past history,
nor the excesses that typified the historical novel as practiced in other countries. If his work is more palatable than
Scott's, this is so largely because it was conceived with
totally different and far deeper awareness of the serious
obligations Manzoni felt a novelist should have toward
the problem of history itself. "It seems to me," he wrote
to Cesare D'Azeglio, "that poetry . . . must try in every
one of its subjects to discover [both] the historical and
moral truth, not only as its goal but as a fuller and more
continuous source of the beautiful; since in both orders of
things, the false [fiction] can amuse, to be sure, but such
delight, such interest, is destroyed by the knowledge of
truth and [is] therefore temporary and accidental. . . .
The historical and moral truth is more alive and stable as
the mind sampling it is more advanced in its perception of
truth."

In a lengthy "Letter to M. Chauvet," (1820) Manzoni
had clearly outlined his ideas about fiction and poetry, and
expressed his opinion that art should not only be intelligible to the common man, but its subject should be drawn
from history which, as he stated, would ultimately be
illuminated by poetry. His meditations on a question close
to his heart led him to the realization that art and truth
were anything if not inseparable companions: "Art," he
wrote, "should have truth as its objective and the interesting as its means." In his view, imaginative writing could
indeed be turned into an excellent instrument to probe
reality itself. Manzoni never intended that the poet
should take over what is a historian's domain, but insisted

that a poet could, by way of his special intuition and sensibility, illuminate the causes and effects of human actions left unexplored by the science of history. The poet, he believed, could not only penetrate history and its secrets; it could make them alive. "To collect the characteristic traits of a period of society and develop them in action," he wrote to Fauriel in January, 1821, apropos Tommaso Grossi's projected epic poem *Longobardi crociati*, "and profit by history, without trying to rival it— that, it seems to me, is something that can still be accorded to poetry, and what alone it can do." Thus, as we can plainly see, Manzoni defined the novelist's goal as twofold: amusement, to be sure, but amusement made meaningful by enlightment and education. He also perceived that in drama—and, by extension, in fiction—the artist should strive to satisfy both the reader's interest in characterization and representation, *and* his natural curiosity in wanting to know "what is really true and to see as much as possible into ourselves and our destiny on earth." It might well be that he chose history as the proper place in which he could locate his fictitious tale simply because it offered experiences and a reality accessible to all, and as such not subject to extensive doubts as to its veracity. He specifically chose the seventeenth century as the time for his tale to unfold partly because of its chonological proximity to his own readers, partly because of the similarities of its socio-political conditions with the nineteenth century's, and perhaps also partly (according to Alberto Moravia) "because then, for the last time, Catholicism informed all Italian life."

It is one of the recognized qualities of the novel that historical and invented events are judiciously mingled and treated with an equal amount of irony which was the product of the author's serenity and detachment. It is, to some extent, thanks to the way the two parts are held together and made into a whole that permits the reader to be less interested in seeing the story resolved than in reading it as an account of how man, not Divine Providence, is to blame for the corrupt and chaotic conditions of his world. A moral vision, firmly founded upon religious principles to which Manzoni adhered without reservations, is thus made concrete through the representation of facts and fancy. This was, as the novel limpidly attests, Manzoni's special formula for putting down on paper, as a poet, what he knew to be historically accurate, and what his religious convictions told him to be true beyond doubt.

Manzoni's readers can hardly miss the significant part religion plays in all of his writings. In a letter to Fauriel, seizing still another opportunity to discuss his important treatise *Osservazioni sulla morale cattolica* (London, 1836; *A Vindication of Catholic Morality or a Refutation of the charges brought against it by Sismondi in his History*) which had just appeared in print, the novelist stated: "Religion only wishes to lead us to wisdom and moderation without unnecessary pain, only to take us by tranquil reflection to that reasonableness which we reach by weariness or by a kind of desparation." Yet, the contradiction between history and religion—or reason and faith—was to leave its indelible mark upon the novel. "Stripped to its essential," comments Mr. Colquhoun, "the dualism of the book is between a religion which reposes all hopes for a just and happy life in the next world, and the rationalism which satirically, acidly hints that the responsibility of a limited class not only aggravates injustices, war, famine and plague, but in essence causes them." Another formidable achievement of *The Betrothed* is its capacity to reconcile and balance Manzoni's genuine respect for history (a respect attested by the numerous readings in history, law, and economics he completed in preparation for the novel) with his religious beliefs. In the end, we perceive that the message of the tale is never allowed to obfuscate or damage the invented parts of the narrative.

History, as we will see, receives a good deal of attention on the part of the author, especially since it serves him to dramatize the great theme of good and evil that is at the center of the story. Indeed, so replete with implications is the conflict, that recent Marxist critics have chosen to interpret it as a brilliant example of class struggle, with the poor, exploited peasants continually at odds with the powerful, rich, and ruthless rulers. Vitally concerned with his theme as Manzoni was, he chose to give it life by examining its roots in human history. The result was an impressive and shocking analysis of the very materials that go into the making of society, and ultimately determine the solidity of the edifice of human relations and feelings. Certainly Manzoni entertained the belief that, fundamentally speaking, man is a corruptible but also a decent rational animal. Nonetheless, there is ample evidence pointing to the fact that his idealistic conception of life was tempered by his awareness that the intricate network of laws enacted to uphold peace and order, are frequently manipulated by the ruling class for the sole purpose of aggrandizing its power, or satisfying its otherwise unjustifiable ambitions at the expense of the weak. As Manzoni's chief Italian biographer Alfredo Galletti observes, "the juice of the whole tale is that, in terrestrial affairs, justice is a myth; that laws are made to hurt the naïve to the advantage of the rascals; and that, on the whole, the world is ruled with as much wisdom as can be found in one of Fra Galdino's walnuts. The official representatives of law and society cut no better figure, except for Cardinal Federigo. Lawyers and magistrates, mayors and councillors, police and military, are either servile or corrupt." Living as we are in an era of political, social, and ideological turmoil, of mass demonstrations staged by minority groups desperately fighting to gain the dignity and the rights long denied them, Manzoni's world seems far from being unreal or improbable.

The world, so somberly depicted by Manzoni's imagination as one both cruel and wicked, is partly redeemed by an intense religious feeling informing the novel and allowing the protagonists to live with, and even accept, their condition. If Renzo, Lucia, and Agnese can survive their ordeal, it is because they are assisted by Providence, a mysterious, pervasive force through which God makes His presence felt to His children. Providence, frequently mentioned as though it were a magical force and yet profusely acknowledged by the heroes for enabling them to keep body and soul together, is what gives hope in this life. "Living [in this novel]," Mario Sansone perceptively writes, "consists no longer in wanting to die, but in accepting the law of life, and operating within such a law for the greatest benefit of all . . . God is here—at once the secret and the [very] reason of Life itself." Without the direct intervention of Providence itself, some of the story's most crucial events could neither take place nor be understood in their full significance. Providence sends Fra Cristoforo to help the two betrothed, just as it acts on a treacherous brigand, the Unnamed, moving him first to pity toward Lucia when he hears her imploring words, then to repentance for a life of crimes committed up to that moment, and finally to his conversion to Catholicism. Providence, too, is what brings Fra Cristoforo to his dramatic confrontation with Don Rodrigo, and gives him the strength to utter words whose impact will not be felt until the closing pages of the book. When he realizes that the bully does not wish to listen to the voice of reason and compassion, he shouts,

> I pity this house. A curse hangs over it. You will see if the justice of God can be kept out by a few stones, or frightened off by a pair of sentries. You think God made a creature in His own image in order to give you the pleasure of tormenting her! You think God won't be able to defend her! You've spurned His warning. You are judged for it! Pharaoh's heart was as hard as yours, and God found a way to crush it. Lucia is safe from you: I—a poor friar—I tell you that; and as far as for yourself, listen to what I foretell you. A day will come.

His ominous prediction proves to be accurate, and Don Rodrigo, the chief cause of much anguish and sorrow, dies a horrible death, as does his henchman Griso—both struck by the plague that is another symbolic manifestation of God's ways.

Renzo, returning to his own town from Milan, exhausted by a perilous and long journey, thinks that he is lost. He finds a small shed in the woods, and decides to spend the night there. Before retiring, he kneels down and offers his humble thanks to the Almighty for having guided him to safety. Even Don Abbondio, the cowardly priest, upon learning that Don Rodrigo is finally dead, is ready to acknowledge the beneficial intervention of Providence, in a manner clearly calculated to inject a note of humor into the story while at the same time illuminating still further his character

> Ah! So he's dead, then. He's really gone. . . . Just see, my children, if Providence doesn't get people like that in the end. D'you know, it's a wonderful thing. A great relief for this poor neighborhood. . . . This plague's been a great scourge, my children, but it's also been a great broom: it's swept away certain folk, my children, whom we never thought we'd be rid of any more.

"A high religious feeling," writes Sapegno, "circulates in every part of [Manzoni's] world, penetrates into every event, touches even the most cruel and vile characters. God's intervention in the large and small happenings is always so strong that one can almost touch it with his hand; it is a paternal presence, loving and severe, that palpitates in every thing. . . . In the world [of poor people], sad more than joyful, God's work may be felt above all in the tribulations, in the anxieties, and in those rays of light that open up, suddenly, in the midst of the darkness of anguish and close the door to despair."

One must search the novel, however, to find in capsule form the moral lesson the tale has tried to convey, along with the true meaning of Providence. Renzo and Lucia, reminiscing about their experiences, "came to the conclusion that troubles often come to those who bring them on to themselves, but that not even the most cautious and innocent behavior can ward them off; and that when they come—whether by our fault or not—confidence in God can lighten them and turn them to our improvement. This conclusion, though reached by poor people, has seemed so just to us that we have thought of putting it down here, as the juice of the whole tale." Ever since the book appeared, but more intensely in recent years, many critics have been confounded or irritated by what is obviously meant to be the summation of a complex and long book. By the same token, readers unwilling to suspend their disbelief have remained unpersuaded by the moral of the tale. Yet, lest one is willing to accept the religious and moral foundations on which *The Betrothed* rests, one can hardly begin to understand the book, and even less like it. Ultimately, the major stumbling block that has prevented many readers from seizing the significance of the novel resides in the fact that not many of us believe either in God, or in miracles, or in sudden, mysterious conversions. And Manzoni wrote his work for an audience that firmly believed, because it was living in a pre-Darwinian and pre-Freudian era, that our real life begins the moment we die. Thus, everywhere in *The Betrothed* psychology is subordinated to, or placed after, religion, and reality is forced, in the words of Moravia, "into the ideological framework of Catholicism." And, because of it, the book betrays its conservative stance, its sympathy toward the *status quo*, its lack of confidence in the ability of man to redeem himself socially, with or without the help of his religion, and fulfill himself as a human being.

Intimately acquainted with the classics of literature of Western Europe as Manzoni was, it is inevitable that echoes of the authors he knew so well and loved so deeply should be found in *The Betrothed*. Indeed, so numerous are his literary debts, ranging from casual borrowing of incidental details to overt reminiscences of episodes and characters, that his major work has frequently lent itself to be studied less for its worth as a poetic expression, than for its sources. Although English was not one of his languages, he was a devoted reader of Shakespeare ("My Shakespeare!" he once said with affection, "Anyone writing poetry must read Shakespeare; how he knows all the feelings!"), and of many English novelists whose works had reached the Italian shores in French translations: Goldsmith, Defoe, Sterne, Walpole, and, of course, Scott. ("Had there not been a Walter Scott," he once confessed to his friend C. Fabris, "the idea of writing a novel would not have occurred to me.") As a faithful student of France, it was natural that he should feel the magnetic attraction of a literature he loved and esteemed so highly. His readings in French were as numerous as they were diversified. They included the chief Renaissance writers, particularly Rabelais and Montaigne; the moralists Bossuet, La Bruyère, Pascal, and La Rochefoucauld; the Encyclopedists Voltaire and Diderot; and the playwrights of the golden age of French theater, Corneille, Racine and Molière. But if *The Betrothed* contains more than a hint of these and numerous other writers, the links one might establish between the classics and our novelist matter little. For he succeeded in fusing his extraordinary readings with his own original and cultured outlook, absorbing the insights of his authors and making them his, coloring them with a special light and refashioning them into something new. Everything he learned, through his studies, observations, and meditation, was carefully filtered through his sensibility and molded, transformed into something that bore the stamp of his personal genius.

The technique Manzoni employed to introduce and narrate his story may serve as a pertinent illustration of the foregoing remarks. There was really nothing novel about his technique, for it has frequently been used before, by Sterne and Walpole among others. But in the hands of the Milanese, it achieves a new, meaningful dimension: it not only gives a special flavor to the book, but becomes an important structural element, giving rise to certain tensions without which the novel would be far less convincing and effective. In his preface Manzoni tells us how he had found "a faded and scratched manuscript," written by an "Anonymous Chronicler." Irked by its awkward, ungrammatical style, he was nevertheless so captivated by the "beautiful story," it contained that he decided to tell it anew. Mr. Colquhoun calls this "a device . . . to bridge the gap between reality and fiction," an assumption that is probably correct. Manzoni, whose views on the role of poetry in the modern world place him in the category of moralists, became singularly aware of the possibilities his method offered him. Indeed, he perceived in the fiction of the finding of the manuscript the element that would enable him to give a ring of authenticity to the story, while at the same time would provide him with a multiple point of view, from which he could narrate *and* invent a compelling story.

The initial pages of the book do much to reveal the nature of the perspectives and roles open to Manzoni. In the first place, his job is to retell a story that is not his own. In a vague sense, his position may be compared to that of a medieval scribe, patiently recopying, in the silence of his cell, an original manuscript. But, as was common with many such copyists, Manzoni immediately takes certain, and admittedly extreme, liberties with his text. As a matter of fact, he edits it in the modern sense of rewriting it *in toto*, for the sake of improving its otherwise unbearably rough style. Not satisfied with recasting the story in his own language, he also adds a number of important passages to the original manuscript. Such sections, judiciously interpolated in the book, are always and clearly identified for what they are—that is, as pages that will illuminate, enrich and clarify the story—written by Manzoni himself. These passages (the most notable of which are to be found in Chapters ix, xxii, xxviii, xxxi, and xxxii) must be viewed as his personal contribution to the artistic whole, and are meant to supply what might be called historical and biographical information not contained in the manuscript. It goes without saying, that the tone changes with the various perspectives, and rightly so: the story is obviously a work of poetry, while the added chapters or paragraphs are the result of the "editor's" special research in the archives. A subtle irony, a gentle humor and an admirable diligence become the salient qualities of the novel, whose parts have been joined harmoniously by a craftsman who never once permits himself any exaggerations. Manzoni's indulgence and patience toward his readers, especially toward those who might experience some irritation when confronted by what may seem digressions, is so great that he seems to apologize for the necessity of such long biographical-historical sections. In one instance (Chapter XXII), he even advises the reader eager to get on with the story, to "skip straight on to the following chapter," a suggestion that can be taken only at the risk of depriving oneself of one of the memorable vignettes in which the novelist excels.

Not content with employing such apparently naïve devices (naïve only if we forget the fact that the novel has all the appearances of a fairy tale) Manzoni injects still another personal note. Time and again, as he is transcribing the story, he meditates on the events just recounted, and makes what must be considered a distinctly ethical or religious judgment on the key issues posed by the actions or words of the characters. And it makes little difference, in the last analysis, whether Manzoni offers the comment as his own, or the Chronicler's, for the effect is quite similar—all the more since we have learned that there is only a thin line dividing the two.

> We cannot forbear pausing a moment to make a reflection in the midst of all this uproar. Renzo, who had raised all this noise in someone else's house, who had got in by a trick, and was now keeping the master of the house himself besieged in a room, has all the appearance of being the aggressor; and yet, if one thinks it out, he was the injured party. Don Abbondio, surprised, terrified, and put to flight while peacefully attending to his own affairs, might seem the victim; and yet, in reality, it was he who was doing the wrong. Such is often the way the world goes . . . I mean, that's the way it went in the seventeenth century.

> Here our anonymous chronicler makes an observation which we repeat for what it is worth. Temperate and honest habits, he says, have this advantage among others, that the more they are settled and rooted in a man, the more sensitive he is to any slight departure from them; so that he remembers it for some time afterwards; and even a folly becomes a useful lesson to him.

It is easy to see, from the two examples taken respectively from Chapters VIII and XIV, how Manzoni, originally committed to transcribing a story he has rewritten in better Italian, frequently betrays the fact that he is also "editing" it, and becomes, by way of his affinity with the moral position of the original narrator, identified with his author. The total effect of a technique that transforms the narrator-commentator into an omniscient seer, is such that it makes us live intimately with the characters, perceiving their aspirations, understanding their frailties as human beings, sympathizing with their plights, and being moved by their situations.

The breadth of vision is matched by an equally astonishing breadth of stylistic virtuosity. Manzoni's sense of language, his exceptional feeling for its possibilities, his inventiveness and versatility are surely among the major achievements of *The Betrothed*. His expressive range is practically limitless: it spans all the way from the lyricism of the passage "Farewell, mountains . . ." (the section being Lucia's adieu to her native ground, at the end of Chapter VIII, a passage regularly committed to memory by all high school students in Italy), to the descriptions of landscapes and feelings, to the incisiveness of his psychological portraits—done with unusual attention to details—to the serene and detached historical passages, whose scholarly seriousness is relieved by touches of light irony. His dialogues and monologues manage to be both vivacious and believable, and their only fault may be a smoothness of diction that may be a bit disconcerting to the reader yearning for a more popular flavor in the characters' speeches. One wishes that Manzoni had made his characters speak in racier, earthier ways, as it befitted their social class. But if the contemporary reader is prone to consider this a disappointing side of the book, he must bear in mind that the author was less preoccupied with rendering his dialogues real in the best sense, than with creating a truly national, literary, and spoken language. In a genuine sense, he was striving for harmony in his style, a harmony that would accompany, or better still translate, his vision of the world.

Harmony is perhaps the one term that helps us under-

stand what must be considered one of the great achievements of the book, certainly insofar as its style was concerned. The concept itself, as descriptive of an ideal goal,
must have meant many things to Manzoni: a spare elegance of diction, a moderate and yet thoughtful narrative
manner that would enable him to carry his story forward
at its just pace. But harmony had also a deeply religious
connotation and meaning: for the poet, it signified a
complete peace attainable by the spirit of a just man, who
accepts the ways of God. Only under such circumstances
can harmony, understood as a perfect rhythm, be visualized as beauty: the man at peace with himself and his
God can be said to have achieved harmony, a vital prereq-
uisite to human happiness. It is this kind of happiness that
is experienced by Lucia or by the Cardinal Borromeo and,
at least at times, by Renzo himself. An artist must also
strive to experience such harmony, for it paves the way to
the perfection—the depth of its whole, the necessity of its
parts, the lucidity of the resulting images—to which he
aspires.

Everything in *The Betrothed* bespeaks of such harmony, and because of it, it conveys an unusual sense of
dignity and of integrity. It was, of course, Manzoni's
meticulousness, his passion for details, that impelled his
admirer Goethe to remark: "*Il eut trop de respect pour la
réalité*" and to suggest that the German translation omit
the lengthier historical passages. Strangely enough, Manzoni approved of the suggestion and dispensed with certain pages depicting the plague of 1630. Nevertheless in
the second version of the book not only did he leave intact
but enlarged what he and others had called the digressions
of the story, thereby sharpening the total effect of the
novel.

In the last analysis, his realism must not be confused
with the technique of the practitioners of the novel in the
second half of the nineteenth century. For Manzoni, his
technique was simply the most apt way to dramatize in
concrete terms what he felt to be an unjust moral order in
seventeenth-century life, based primarily on historical

facts: "I am transcribing," he wrote with his usual modesty, "a story which really happened, and true events proceed with quite other rules to those laid down by imagination. . . . If it were possible to subject these rules to the course desired by poetic spirits, the world would become even more delightful than it is; but that is not a thing that can be hoped. And it is through the fault of this wasteful and material procedure of facts," he concluded, "that Renzo arrives twice in Milan, stays there and leaves, all in rather similar ways."

In his handling of time, Manzoni also took a cautiously historical and eminently traditional approach. Thus, while the novel spans approximately three years, the bulk of its action takes place within a relatively short period of time. Similarly, almost one fifth of what is surely a long novel concerns itself either with an account of the extraordinary lives of certain key characters (Fra Cristoforo, Gertrude the Nun of Monza, Cardinal Borromeo, the Unnamed, and, of course, Don Abbondio) or with certain historical events necessary to understand the implications of the tale and the fate of its heroes.

The story begins the fateful evening of November 7, 1628, when Don Abbondio is met by the *bravoes* sent by Don Rodrigo, and ends three years later, when Renzo and Lucia finally marry and begin having children. Throughout the first twenty-six chapters of *The Betrothed* Manzoni gives us a narrative constructed along strictly controlled chronological lines, even when his references to time are confined to such expressions as the next day, or the previous day. In the second part of the book, which might be said to begin after the great confrontation of Don Abbondio with Cardinal Borromeo, the pace of the novel is considerably stepped up, and entire seasons are practically skipped over in order for the author to focus his attention on the fate of his characters, seen this time in history, rather than acting their little drama before a historical backdrop. Significantly enough, the major encounters between the chief characters—Don Abbondio, Don Rodrigo, Fra Cristoforo, Renzo, Lucia, the Nun of

Monza, the Unnamed and Cardinal Borromeo—occur in the first part of the book. The second part of the novel, on the other hand, is characterized by long historical accounts. The quality of the narrative is determined by the turns the story takes: it is intimate and detailed up to the point when the sinister Unanmed is converted, more detached and ironical afterwards.

We must stand away from the book, and return to it again and again, in order to appreciate fully the complexity of its structure, the richness of its details, the wealth of its anticipatory signals and retrospective illuminations, all these contribute to the diversity and interest of the whole. Few other novelists in modern Italy have so thoroughly mastered Manzoni's exemplary use of the material at his disposal. Fewer still have been able to recreate an era so convincingly as he. Working with an impressive cast of characters, he describes each of them so well—from the protagonists to the lesser figures—that we never find ourselves unable to accept their words or deeds as something not fully consonant with their whole personality. With an Olympian serenity, a tolerant yet penetrating hand, Manzoni delves into the character of his personages without ever forgetting the traits that make them at once strong and weak creatures. His scrutinizing eye by no means confines its gaze to any special social class or to any specific type of individual. Rather, it embraces an extraordinarily broad spectrum of humanity, the rich and the poor, the saintly and the satanic, the educated and the ignorant, the humble and the arrogant, the strong and the weak. A diversified gallery of people—priests, cardinals, monks, soldiers, lackeys, *bravoes*, lawyers, rulers, farmers, adminstrators, lords, *monatti*, workers, bakers—passes under our eyes: "I've stuffed [my novel]," remarked Manzoni, "with peasants, nobles, magistrates, scholars, war, famine . . . that's to have written a book!" There is room for all of them in the story, to be sure. What is amazing is not so much their number, or their diversity, but the fact that once we have met them, it is difficult to forget them. Many of them have become proverbial in Italian life.

"In writing [my] essay on Manzoni," confesses Bernard
Wall on the opening page of his book, "I have felt an old
uneasiness. . . . Is it that in the restlessness and anguish of
the mid-twentieth century Manzoni is too calm, too *enra-
ciné?* . . . At least this can be said. We live in 'abnormal,'
unpredictable times, and Manzoni was in his writing always 'normal.' He was never *damné*, never scintillating,
never paradoxical. His work was a work of common sense,
of pedestrian observation architected to the level of genius." Few Italians would agree with Mr. Wall's characterization of the book, for it is unlikely, if not hazardous, for
them to question the work of a master that has been
institutionalized and transformed, as it were, into a sacred
cow. But doubts have the bad habit of lingering on,
nagging us until they have been intellectually or emotion-
ally resolved, as best befits the situation. Indeed, the question of whether *The Betrothed* must continue being admired either uncritically or without reservations, impelled
the novelist Alberto Moravia to write a long essay that
forms the introduction to the 1961 de luxe edition of the
novel, published by Einaudi of Turin. Space prevents me
from going into a detailed examination of Moravia's rea-
soned, perceptive if highly controversial interpretation. I
urge the reader to get the essay for himself, for he will find
it stimulating to say the least. But Moravia's major points
surely have a large measure of validity, and help us understand more completely the inadequacies of *The Betrothed*.

Moravia's thesis is that Manzoni's work is to a large
extent a "work of propaganda," "an attempt at Catholic
realism." His novel reveals its author's "ambition . . . not
only to represent the whole of Italian reality on a huge
scale, but to force this reality—without distorting or am-
putating it in any unnatural way—into the ideological
framework of Catholicism." The flaws of the entire work
are all directly traceable to such an ambition: thus, for
example, evil in the novel (and we know that the theme
of the book shows us, again and again, the clash that
results when good and evil meet) is never adequately

presented: we know little of why Don Rodrigo or the Unnamed, for example, got to be as wicked as we are told they are; "Manzoni never bothers to explain why or how they are wicked." As a result, the picture we get, whether it concerns people or history, is necessarily partial, since it is explained, *when* it is explained at all, in religious or moral, rather than in social or psychological terms.

From this, it also follows that the conversions from a condition of impulsiveness or evil to one of meekness and goodness, as exemplified by Fra Cristoforo and the Unnamed, remain unconvincing, if only because the first is explained as the result of practical necessity, and the second as a sudden, baffling decision to abandon the old wicked ways—a decision that is not preceded by an internal, profound spiritual turmoil that brings the Unnamed to repentance. We have the disconcerting feeling that the Unnamed is simply afraid to face old age and the impending death with as vile a record as he has achieved. The very problem of his conversion has traditionally been the subject of prolonged polemics and discussions. Here, I am inclined to side with those critics who believe that Manzoni, perhaps unconsciously, projected the mystery of his own conversion, and its irrationality *sui generis* (for as a rule matters of faith do not conveniently lend themselves to rational explanations) into the personal drama of his character. Thus, just as we shall never really know why Manzoni returned to his Church, so we shall never truly understand the reasons why the Unnamed experiences a crisis that changes him from a scoundrel into a saint. Surely he who, after a long life of crimes and violence, becomes the exact opposite of what he has always been without going through a long and tormenting metamorphosis, must be looked upon with the considerable mixture of apprehension and mistrust characterizing poor Don Abbondio's attitude toward him. Perhaps here, too, Manzoni was simply inclined to let God, acting through Providence, save or destroy His creatures: "Man," writes Moravia, "can do nothing against evil; evil has to work itself out to the bitter end: then Providence will take charge in its inscrutable manner so as to save those individuals or societies worthy of salvation."

It is ultimately impossible to do justice to Manzoni's novel unless we bear in mind that he occupied a political, religious, and social position that was conservative, if not reactionary, by today's standards. He composed his masterpiece under the influence of his conversion, wishing to dramatize above everything else the truth of his faith. Thus, while the contemporary reader must not object to a novel that is, in every way, a religious work, he may find himself unsympathetic to Manzoni's implicit exhortation to preserve the *status quo*. Such a reader may also resent the view that only the elect will find salvation, just as he will no doubt disagree with a position that indirectly, but unmistakably, equates poverty with social and intellectual inferiority. But what is possibly the book's most disturbing point, is the lesson that it tries to impart to the reader; to him it is presented as the juice of the whole tale. A truly Christian drama is transformed, in the final lines of the book, into an exhortation to conform and keep still, in the face of injustice.

I suppose that it has been such a combination of factors discussed in the preceding pages that have contributed to making Manzoni at once the most classical and limpid novelist of modern Italy as well as the writer who is not always likely to appeal to the interest and curiosity of the contemporary reader. Why is that? The answer, in part, has been suggested by Mr. Wall: it is simply too difficult, in the chaotic and uncertain world of today, to be intrigued by a novel where hardly anything happens as the result of what we loosely call pure chance. There is far too much serenity in Manzoni's cosmos or in his manner of recounting his tale, and we live in a historical moment that has taught us to expect, not to say fear, the improbable, erratic gesture that may well doom mankind. There are, in *The Betrothed*, far too many happy resolutions: the good people are invariably rewarded, in this life or beyond it, and the bad people are always punished. No one, I assume, objects to the desirability of such a state of affairs, but most will seriously doubt its probability in human life. Unlike Dante, who was also a great Catholic writer, Manzoni simply stacked the cards against those who were faithless and was unable to create in his novel the tension between the human and the Divine judgment that makes the *Comedy* the intensely dramatic and moving experience that it is.

Having said this, we must acknowledge that *The Betrothed* is a significant novel indeed—not merely because of its admirable moral content, or its limpid style, or its use of humble people as heroes of the story and of a regional setting (two factors that anticipate the innovations of the later *verismo*). Despite the passing of time, it remains a candid portrayal of the virtues and flaws of the Italian temperament, the hopefulness and honesty that characterize the masses of Italy, the arrogance and corruption that typify her ruling elite, and the general level of conformity that has traditionally permeated the entire nation. "It is a fact," notes Alberto Moravia, "that Manzoni's novel reflects an Italy which, with few inessential modifications, could be the Italy of today." "To know Italy," concludes Mr. Wall, "we must appreciate Manzoni, but to appreciate Manzoni, I sometimes feel, we must know Italy." Possibly, this is the largest compliment we can pay a writer; and it is hard to think of anyone else in the history of modern Italy whose work has become one with the spirit of the culture which gave it birth.

I was born a Venetian 18 September 1775, the Day of St. Luke the Evangelist and I shall die, by the Grace of God, an Italian, whenever the Providence that mysteriously controls our world shall so ordain.

This is the lesson of my life. But in so far as this lesson was due not to myself but to the times in which I lived, it has occurred to me that a simple account of the influence of those times upon the life of one man could be of some use to those who, in later days, are destined to feel the less imperfect consequences of what has already been achieved.

In this Year of our Lord 1858 I am now aged more than eighty years, though still young at heart . . . I have lived and suffered much, but am no less rich in those consolations that, for the most part, remain unrecognized among the tribulations. . . . My nature, my talent, my early education and the progress of my destiny were, as all things human, a mingling of good and of bad; were it not for the indiscreet quirk of modesty I could also add that, in my own case, the bad was rather more abundant than the good.

I am neither a theologian, nor a learned man, nor a philosopher, and yet I want to give my opinion like a traveler who, however ignorant, can rightly judge whether the land that he has passed through be poor or rich, unpleasant or beautiful. . . . Life is what our nature makes it, that is to say our nature and our upbringing; as physical fact it is a necessity, as a moral fact that is the office of justice. Who by his own temperament will be in all matters just toward himself, toward others, towards all humanity, he will be the most innocent, useful and noble man who has ever passed through this world. His life will be a benefit to himself and

and to all and will leave an honoured and profound mark upon the history of his country. That is the archetype of a real and perfect man. What matters if others live afflicted and unhappy? They are the degenerates, the strayed, the guilty. . . . Happiness is in our consciences; bear that well in mind. The certain proof of our spiritual life, wherever it may be, resides in justice.

These two excerpts, whose moral, patriotic, and philosophical implications can hardly escape the attention of the reader, serve respectively to introduce and conclude the confessions of Carlo (Carlino, as he is called in his younger days) Altoviti, the eighty-three-year-old narrator-protagonist of *Le confessioni di un italiano* (Boston, 1958; *The Castle of Fratta*), one of the truly engaging, colorful, and adventureous novels of the nineteenth century. Its author was Ippolito Nievo who, at the age of thirty (at the time of the completion of his book) had already behind him a promising literary production and a distinguished career as a civil servant. In his historical narrative, *Dal Quarto al Volturno*, Cesare Abba describes him with these telling words: "A Venetian poet, who at the age of twenty-eight has written novels, ballads, and tragedies. He will be the poet-soldier of the expedition. Sharp profile, genius shining on his brows. A striking figure. A fine soldier." The epithet of poet-soldier eventually stuck and, as Miss Olga Ragusa correctly remarks, "critical opinion on Nievo, the writer, thus crystallized on non-literary elements." Anyone who has studied him is bound to feel attracted by Nievo's ability to feel intensely, with a mixture of joy and sadness, about life, or by his seemingly inexhaustible appetite for the tragicomedy of existence. Indeed, it must have been this side of the novelist's personality that impelled Sergio Romagnoli to write, in his splendid Introduction to the 1952 Ricciardi edition of Nievo's *Opere*: "there is no Italian writer who, within a thirty-year span, accomplished an equal amount of work, without denying himself life itself—that is, family affections, love, study, friendships, walks, fighting in politics and in wars alike."

For all the dash and exuberance informing his master-piece, and despite its originality and worth as a historical novel encompassing events of great magnitude and drama, neither the book nor its author have commanded steady attention among the critics and readers. Although the first monograph on Nievo was brought out at the turn of the century, even an acceptable edition of his main literary production had to wait until the early fifties before ap-pearing. Interest in Nievo seems to have gained considera-ble momentum shortly before the outbreak of World War II. Part of this interest was generated by the reappraisals of past works that take place periodically as the result of changes in taste; but much of it probably is traceable to the magnetism of *The Castle of Fratta*. After all, what is unusual about being absorbed by a book that speaks to us about consequential matters—what we are, how did we become this way, and where are we going? The main purpose of his book is to give us a feeling of the anguish, the struggles, and the combination of victories and set-backs experienced by a nation on its way to independence. But the political-historical theme of the book is closely interwoven with a love story, the grand passion of the protagonist for his elusive cousin Pisana. It is easy to see, even on the basis of such general characterization, why *The Castle of Fratta*, much like Pasternak's *Doctor Zhi-vago* and Lampedusa's *The Leopard*, should be enjoying a favorite position in today's Italy. The extraordinary suc-cess encountered by this particular type of narrative, which according to critical consensus often gives a dis-torted or at best a partial interpretation of history, must simply be ascribed to an all too-human longing to read a story set in less complex, if only deceptively less painful, times than the ones we live in. This is even truer, I believe, when as in the case of Nievo, the writer exhibits what Miss Ragusa calls "a nostalgia of a dead world," accompanied by "fervent hopes for the future." The pa-thos of the novel is always restrained and nicely balanced by the engaging vitality of the adventureous tale it tells. It is no wonder that some critics, notably the late Ernest H.

Wilkins, have considered *The Castle of Fratta* "the one great novel of the [post-Manzoni] period."

Two main reasons have been offered as partial explanations, if not justification, of the neglect long endured by Nievo: the inordinate length of his chief novel, which runs close to a half million words, thus ranking as one of the longest single stories ever written by an Italian, and the adverse evaluation offered by the influential Benedetto Croce, whose objections to our author and his work proved to be effective enough to influence an entire generation of readers. The notable shortcomings of the Nievian masterpiece—its length, its grammatical flaws unpardonable in a country that places a heavy premium on stylistic elegance, the rambling character of the entire second part—may have been due less to the author's sensitivity or temperament than to what we may simply call his working habits. Nievo composed his book at an almost compulsive pace, writing it feverishly between December 1857 and mid-August 1858. He refused to allow enough time to elapse so that he might refashion his novel into something more tightly constructed. Internal evidence indicates that he revised only the first half of his manuscript, without bothering to eliminate a good many pages that make his story unwieldy, distracting the reader's interest from the central themes and figures. He poured entirely too much into his book (at least one critic has complained that it contains enough material for several novels), and the richness of his story possibly contributed both to "the bad design of the book" (the words are Croce's) and to the unevenness of the narrative. The complexity of the tale is unquestionably the factor that caused the insufferable *coups de scène* and the numerous *deus ex machina*, without which the tangled plot could never be resolved. Finally, Nievo was unable to see his novel through the press, for the work that was to consign his name to posterity did not appear until six years after his death.

It is clear that Nievo never allowed his artistic ambitions to interfere with the demands of practical life. Indeed, what we know about him points to a man unwilling to trade action for meditation, incapable of abandoning the field of battle for the tranquillity and safety of his ivory tower. In the mid-1800's when his country was fighting to achieve political independence, Nievo was quick to respond to the call of duty. He put on his uniform and participated in two campaigns; the first, in 1859, against the hated Austrians; the second, in 1860–61, as a member of Garibaldi's Thousand, fighting against the Bourbons. After the departure of Garibaldi's militia from Sicily, Nievo left for Naples where he was to take up a new post. A short time later, he was ordered to return to Palermo; a month later, on March 4, 1861, having completed his assignment, he sailed for Naples on the *Ercole*. The vessel never reached the destination, but was lost at sea; whether it was shipwrecked or destroyed by fire has never been ascertained. Nievo, along with eighty passengers and crew members, lost his life while still in his prime. His existence, brief as it had been, bespeaks of his deep desire to be, in the truest sense, an artist at the service of his country. "He sang of his period as a poet," notes Joseph Spencer Kennard, "lived through it as a soldier, and described it in his masterpiece. His life, his novel, his Italy, are typical; each explains the other."

The very richness and variety of content to which I have alluded would not, in themselves, be reasons enough to single out *The Castle of Fratta*. The originality of the book, whose sweeping quality makes one think of *War and Peace, La Chartreuse de Parme,* and *The Betrothed*, lies in quite another direction. More freely than others, and with a more authentic personal stamp, the book fuses autobiographical and invented material to give us a picture that has a human and a historical significance. It is irrelevant to discuss, in the present context, the similarity of the hero and heroine of the story with the author and his cousin Bice Melzi, for what matters is that they are believable, and entirely captivating figures, endowed with a personality that permits them to live independently of their author. The novelty of the book is, first of all, in the vivacity and realism of its characters, but also, and perhaps principally, in the way in which they assume the role of protagonists in the drama that is political and human. To be sure, even without being Romantic in the strictest sense, Nievo implicitly accepted the notion of fiction as a vehicle to inculcate a moral truth, and as demonstration on the level of poetry of a way of life that could be just and compassionate at the same time. But he also transcended his literary tradition in several important respects. Firstly, he shows us a man of humble birth who becomes the Italian who narrates his own story as well as that of his country; secondly, he identifies his narrator protagonist with the citizen of the new Italy, capable of detachedly looking at recent past history and extracting a lesson from it for future action; thirdly, he endows his creatures with enviable strength and courage of conviction to fight their own battles. Of the dozens of historical novels written in the nineteenth century, and justly consigned to oblivion, *The Castle of Fratta* has withstood the test of time, because, as the literary historian Natalino Sapegno observes, "the historical theme is no longer born out of the impulse of fashion, it does not respond to external reasons or aesthetic preferences, [but] is, rather, the expression of a new and active culture that wants to acquire an awareness of itself and of its tradition." Unlike his predecessors, Nievo was candid enough to deal with the truth as *he* saw it, as a patriot and as a novelist, debunking, whenever necessary, public or private myths. In his novel, both Napoleon and the poet-novelist Ugo Foscolo, at once the idols and the devils of public imagination, find themselves satirized and justly cut down to size, as it were. Of course, it is true that the irony and effectiveness of the book are due to the fact that the hero of the story is the narrator, protagonist, and recorder of past events, and therefore amply entitled to a multiplicity of perspective possible in such cases. This permits a certain amount of moralizing, or commentary, on events being described, but the reader finds himself more willing to tolerate them since they come from the mouth of one who has undergone the experience narrated. We might notice that, when compared with his most illustrious predecessor, Manzoni, what is striking about Nievo, in terms of his attitude, is his willingness to show how history is the true product of man, his blunders or foresight, not of Providence. Therefore, history can neither be exalted nor disparaged, for the hope it generates is determined only by the men who are its architects. But what is particularly novel is Nievo's emphasis on the possibilities of change through wars and revolutions, through which the individual will gain greater freedom and his country will achieve new dignity in the family of nations.

Nievo's choice of the historical setting for his novel was suggested, on the one hand, by his life experiences (the story is set in the author's native ground and covers at least a portion of a period he had witnessed), and, on the other hand, by his strong commitment to his times. In *The Castle of Fratta* we are not transported into the world of a past more or less wretched, or a world whose remoteness enables the novelist to take certain liberties with history, distorting it when necessary to sustain the cogency of the plot. Nor are we asked to see and study his characters from afar, with the objectivity possible when the narrator is not one with the protagonist. On the contrary, we mingle with them in the privacy of their abodes; we travel in their company, journeying to far away cities or nations; we constantly feel the pulsation of their activities. History, to be sure, remains quite important for Nievo, as it had been for Manzoni and the majority of his followers and epigones. But history as he presents it shows people in an earthly pilgrimage, during which they experience love, war, sorrow, pain, sickness, and loneliness before they fulfill their human destinies. When we reach the end of the hero's long confessions, we are not at all surprised to find, as in Manzoni's novel, that the protagonist gives us a summation of the lesson he has learned through his experiences. What we do not find in Carlino's words, however, is an expression of his faith in the power of a benevolent God who, acting through Divine Providence, has either punished or rewarded His children. Without being a religious, Carlino accepts the inevitability of good and evil in the world, while at the same time he points out man's capacity to work out his destiny by exercising his free will. Nowhere better than in the respective attitudes of Manzoni's and Nievo's principal characters do we get a feeling of their world view: thus, where Renzo would imply that noninvolvement is the safest path to perfect happiness (his final words are nothing less than a promise to stay out of trouble, not to make speeches in the streets, and "a hundred things of the kind"—advice that if followed could only lead down the path of servitude and tyranny), Carlino, by his words and deeds, upholds the necessity of being committed. "Happiness is in our consciences," he humbly states toward the end of the book, and we must accept his words as yet another expression of the individual attempt each man must make to reach it, as best as his powers permit. Carlino is sufficiently wise to be aware that he has attained only an imperfect understanding of himself (and therefore a limited amount of happiness and fulfillment), for the world is inscrutable, a large enigma to the mind of a finite being. Moreover, whatever he has learned by the end of his long and rich life, replete with all sorts of experiences, can hardly transcend its private significance, even when the lessons he has mastered gave an undeniable degree of universal applicability.

If, as I have hinted, the spirit of the novel is distinctly Romantic, so obvious is Nievo's penchant for adventure, color, and love-story telling, his sensitivity is more modern than chronology would normally lead us to believe. Carlino's remembrance of things past, his vivid recreation of the life in his native town which has since his birth decayed and all but died (something that permits him to repeat the *où sont les neiges d'antan* motif) has inclined some critcs to speak of him as a kind of Proust *avant la lettre*. Nievo's harking back to his childhood experiences as vital to a valid understanding of the complexity of his existence and the inexorability of his loneliness may make us think of the later psychological novelists. Even in his attitude toward history, as we have seen, Nievo's stance is more modern than that of the majority of his contemporaries. "Nothing of all this would be unusual or worth telling," he frankly confesses at one point, except "that an account of my experience will serve as an example of those countless individual destinies that, from the breaking up of old political orders to the refashioning of the present one, together compose the great national destiny of Italy." Not until De Roberto, almost forty years later, will we find an equal eagerness to study seriously recent historical events as one possible way to understand the present, thus gaining some insights into the problems brought about by the Risorgimento and by the eventual unification of the country.

Both in terms of treatment and theme, *The Castle of Fratta* is an ambitious book. It purports to give us an incisive, accurate, and complete (at least insofar as the memory of its protagonist permits) picture of pre-Risorgimento Italy, and of the first wars of independence. Within the limitations of the fictional story it tells, it also analyzes the political maneuverings and deals, as well as the military defeats that bore their fruit only in the second half of the nineteenth century. The novel spans from 1780 to 1858, and passes in review the central historical events of that period. Nonetheless, by virtue of the fact that the protagonist is also the narrator-author, his figure occupies a focal position, from which everything that happens is observed and interpreted. More convincingly than in Manzoni's *The Betrothed*, history becomes in Nievo's novel the very stuff of the lives of the characters, the experience that involves them all, if in varying degrees. Indeed, in this respect Nievo is considerably more successful than his predecessor, for he makes history the very fabric of the book, and at last the characters have the opportunity to operate in and upon it, less by accident or fate than choice. Stated in another way, the novel might be characterized as a journey from the sheltered world of the castle to the chaotic, but infinitely rich world of history, a method that permits the author to depict the collapse of an era, and the slow, painful but inevitable emergence of another. Throughout this journey, that takes Carlino Altoviti from boyhood to old age, most of the characters fulfill their destinies as lovers and as protagonists in the historical drama of their era: indeed, history and love serve as the elements of tension without which the tale would be deprived of its effectiveness and interest.

In the last analysis, the novel's special character is the profoundly moving and intriguing richness of human experience it recounts, so that its pace is determined not by history itself, but by the love story of three couples, all of whom are destined to meet with a different fate: Carlino and Pisana; her sister, Countless Clara, and doctor Lucilio Vianello; and Leopardo Provedoni and Doretta. As befits the character of the book, which is of the confessional variety, the three couples do not receive an equal amount of attention, even if their stories are masterfully developed to their resolution. The destiny of each character is followed strictly from the perspective of the protagonist, and whatever happens to them is seen and evaluated in terms of Carlino's and Pisana's lives.

At the opening of the story, Carlino is barely seven, two years older than his cousin Pisana. For several chapters, which are the most vivid and important of the book, we are locked in the atmosphere of the forbidding, yet enormously fascinating castle. We learn of Carlino's background from the lips of an old and devoted servant, the cheese grater Martino, under whose benevolent eyes the two youngsters grow up, dreaming, playing, getting into mischief, experiencing their first adventures and sorrows. We also witness the last siege of the castle of Fratta, in 1786, which in retrospect is presented as the event marking the beginning of the decline not only of Fratta, but of the whole Venetian Republic. We then move to Padua (Nievo's native city) where Carlino enrolls in the School of Jurisprudence, and where he remains until 1792. The political atmosphere of Europe, meanwhile, is drastically and irrevocably changing. At one point Nievo writes,

"France had decapitated a king and abolished the monarchy. . . . Alliances and treaties were being concluded on
every side . . . the old Europe, aroused from its sleep by a
blood-stained ghost, struggled to exercise it." Yet the Republic of Venice cannot read the handwriting on the wall
and chose a "null and ruinous policy of unarmed neutral-
ity." The arrival of Napoleon, in 1796, fires the imagination of the young liberals, who entertain the hope that the
dictator might begin making the unification of Italy possible. Their illusion, however, is short-lived, for Venice and
its territories are eventually traded at Campoformio in a
treacherous political deal between Napoleon and the Austrians. During a brief interlude, Carlino manages to return
to the castle and restore order there, winning the admira-
tion and gratitude of the populace which names him their
avogadore.

About midway in the book, we suddenly learn that
Calino's father, long thought to be dead, is very much
alive: he makes a quick entrance into his son's world, and
pledges to help him realize his political ambitions. With
his help, in fact, Carlino on May 1, 1797, is elected to the
Great Council of the Republic of Venice as a voting
Patrician. The political situation has further deteriorated,
as "all Italy dirtied its knees behind the triumphal footsteps of Bonaparte, who deceived one and mocked another with alliances, flatteries and half measures." And
Venice soon ceases being an autonomous state, while Carlino, whose youth is now behind him, becomes a political
exile, and begins many pilgrimages that will see him visiting several cities in Italy and abroad.

But what of the other characters? Countess Clara, is
described at the beginning of the book as "being a believer
. . . devout and fervent, since her faith was not enough,
. . . she wanted love also." A marvelously gracious and
melancholy figure, she cannot marry Lucio, desperately in
love with her, because family traditions do not permit
such a union. She resigns herself to entering a convent,
but Lucio will continue loving her, hoping against hope
that some day she might accept his affection. Pisana,

lively, flirtatious, volatile, has acceded to her old mother's request that she marry Count Mauro Navagèro, a peevish old man whose money will help the family's dwindling estate. Bored with her husband, she runs to Carlino until he is forced to go into exile; later on, she betrays the Count with her *cavaliere servente*, a dashing French officer who disappoints her by refusing to betray his country for her. Once again, she is with Carlino (now thirty-years old), whom she persuades to marry Aquilina Provedoni, a young girl with whom he is in love.

An extraordinary number of adventures, which make the characters appear and disappear almost magically, see Carlino in trouble several times: when Napoleon is overthrown, Carlino joins the liberal forces of Guglielmo Pepe, is wounded and taken prisoner, and finally sentenced to the gallows. Through the intervention of Pisana, he is dramatically saved. Having contracted ophthalmia in the Gaeta jails and barred from Italy, Carlino goes to London. He is joined by Pisana who is anxious to care for him, as he is now nearly blind from cataracts. The greater part of the final chapters are permeated with so much pathos that they border on a sentimentality of the worst sort. For we see Pisana forced to work to support the protagonist by embroidering, sewing, and even begging in the streets. Fortunately, fate is for a little while kind to the two lovers. Thanks to an operation to remove the cataracts, performed by Lucilio who has been living in London for some time, Carlino's eyesight is restored. Now he must witness the death of Pisana, whose strength has literally been sapped by the strenuous existence she has led, by the unfriendliness of the people, and the wretchedness of the climate.

As for the last couple, Leopardo and Doretta, surely theirs is a story of a stormy, sensual, and even senseless passion. For it is clear from the very moment they meet, that the two are hardly compatible in temperament, background, or sensitivity. True enough, we must imagine for ourselves the steady and irreparable deterioration of their marriage, the gruesome metamorphosis of two lovers into two wretched people. But we are given an intimation of their final break when Nievo speaks of Doretta as "arrogant and corss-grained, was discontented with everything; her husband, always hoodwinked and irritated with her, was unjust and cruel in turn." Doretta will ultimately become the mistress of a Don-Juan, the castellan Raimondo ("It was the task of the young castellan to calm her after [her] rages, and how he succeeded and to what honour of the credulous Leopardo, I leave it to my readers to guess"), and Leopardo will commit suicide, incapable of bearing his wife's adultery. The scene of his final hours of agony, after he takes poison, is haunting and deeply moving. Carlino, as Leopardo's friend, is asked to keep him company until death will take him away from the unbearable sufferings of life.

Only in his later years, thanks to a greatly changed political climate, can Carlino return to his beloved Italy. The pages that tell us of the end of his exile are few, and the narrative moves briskly toward its conclusion. Carlino spends his remaining years reminiscing on the past, noting the death of several great figures, and witnessing the first underground movements and the ensuing wars against Austria. He settles down to write his memoirs, inserting in his book sections from the diary of a son, who has gallantly died in South America, fighting for the freedom of far-away nations.

The novel is too stuffed with historical facts for me to do it justice; its episodes are both varied and diverse, and Nievo succeeds in recreating a stormy period less as a historian than as a poet. For his book, unlike history, gives us a real feeling for things as they were and how they have changed. It enables us, above all, to see the unfolding of momentous events from a perspective that is at once subjective and objective, since the action is viewed in retrospect by a man who was part of it. And the tone, for the same reasons, is discursive, intimate and, not infrequently, lyrical. It would be inconceivable, of course, to think of a Nievo without Manzoni preceding him, yet, as I have tried to show, the differences by far outnumber the similarities. Thus, for example, Carlino and Pisana differ from Manzoni's Renzo and Lucia by seeming to be capable of leading a fully authentic life, buffeted by fate, to be sure, but never its willing victims. They are enterprising, imaginative, and resourceful; endowed with a strong character, they can be realistic or idealistic as the case requires. "Everyone knows that Providence matures her designs through our own thoughts, our own sentiments, and our own works," Carlino comments wisely at one point, "and to hope to receive food from her already cooked was either a dream of the desperate or the flattery worthy only of street women." Man, as the novelist seems to assume, is put on earth to fulfill a mission he shall never fully comprehend until the curtain is about to fall for the last time on the stage. Yet he, and he alone, must work that mission out for himself, fighting against all odds, if necessary, so as to conquer his own dimension and place in history. "Manzoni's characters," writes Nicolae Iliescu, "while supremely human, move, in a certain sense, within a well-defined scheme of thought. . . . In Nievo, instead, each character . . . moves in a spacious field of action, thoughts and sentiments without that sense of rational inevitability that gives importance and singularity to Manzoni's characters."

As a novelist working within a young and unadventurous narrative tradition, Nievo depends for his effort purely on characterization and plot. It has often been observed that, had he had the time and opportunity to revise his manuscript, he might have produced a book with a more limpid story, less marred by occasional awkwardness or confusion, or by stylistic gracelessness. It is doubtful that additional time or work could have improved the collection of characters he created to inhabit his book; they constitute indeed a veritable gallery of human beings who are as real as any that sprung from the pen of an Italian. The two major figures of Carlino and Pisana are drawn with the depth, sympathy, and completeness possible to a novelist who models his creatures on himself and on people he has intimately known and understood. Both are vivaciously and coherently developed. Perhaps one of the notable qualities of the narrative is to be found precisely in the manner in which Nievo transforms Carlino, a playful and dreaming boy, into an idealistic, brave, and adventuresome man, at once reflective and generous; Pisana, a fickle, capricious, and spoiled young girl, on the other hand, matures into a woman capable of great passion and sacrifices, never losing her thirst for happiness to be found outside conventions. The supporting cast is equally colorful; but more than that, it lends a special dimension to the narrative through its variety. Clara and Vianello, together with Leopardo and Doretta, for example, aptly complement the two protagonists's romantic and idyllic love. To be sure, as Natalino Sapegno remarks, Leopardo's passion for Doretta betrays its literary inspiration; still, it lends to the novel a pathetic, almost tragic, note that adds further resonance to the tale.

The lesser characters filling the huge canvas of the Nievian world are as large in number as they are memorable: there is the old, kind Martino, who exerts considerable influence upon the young Carlino; there is also Spaccafumo, Captain Sandracca (the commander of an outdated and ineffectual militia), the Dowager Countess (it is impossible to forget her quasi-royal descents to the castle's cavernous kitchen to give the orders for the day), her old husband, the Signor Count, with his boots, spurs, and sword dangling at his side; there is also his fat, hypocritical gourmand brother, Monsignor Orlando, embodying the worst features of a politically reactionary and morally corrupt church; there is Carlino's father, a clever yet generous merchant who seems to make his entrances at the right moment; and, finally, there is a myriad of soldiers, servants, politicians, captains, administrators—all of them enable the story to proceed at its almost impetuous pace, giving it a brio that adds to the warmth of its composition.

Through the action of Carlino, who finds himself in the midst of history and accepts his role in what is clearly a new society, Nievo also conveys a sense of the passing of time, the changes it brings to the seasons of mankind, altering its directions, shaping its sensibility. At the end of an extraordinarily long, and equally rich book, no reader can possibly doubt that Nievo's avowed intention of dealing with "the live and boiling matter . . . of a man's life" has amply been fulfilled. As Carlino himself looks back to a life that has known action and reflection love and suffering, comedy and tragedy, now that he has reached the end of his adventurous pilgrimage, he can serenely declare, "The calm of my soul is forever undisturbed, like the calm of a sea where there are no winds; I march towards death as towards a mystery, obscure and inscrutable, yet deprived for me of menaces and fears." We should look to such a declaration if we wish to find the secret of Nievo's modernity; for here we find a man with the courage of his convictions, at peace with himself and even happy as he examines his past, for he knows he has done his best—and his best is equated not with withdrawal from life for the sake of personal safety, but with a strong determination to be himself, never refusing to be engaged in the challenges, variety, and surprises life has in store for man.

4   EMILIO DE MARCHI:
THE PATHOS OF EXISTENCE

RARELY DO WE FIND in the history of the nineteenth-
century novel in Italy a world as complex as that of
Alessandro Manzoni, or one inhabited by as rich an assort-
ment of characters from all social strata as one encounters
in the pages of *The Betrothed*. Nevertheless, it is instructive to turn from Manzoni to a celebrated Manzoniano,
Emilio De Marchi, for his work offers not only a startling
contrast to that of his maestro, but a fine example of a
reorientation of certain novelists toward a depiction of a
more contemporary society. In the fiction of De Marchi
we move to a simpler world whose central problem is to
find, amidst frustrating circumstances, a modicum of happiness. As Miss Kathleen Speight has noted, De Marchi's
"typical characters are the most ordinary, normal, everyday folk of these [the middle and working] classes; office
workers, cobblers, millers, parish priests, peasants, farm
labourers, market women; people living very common-
place, monotonous, humdrum and struggling lives . . .
who accept their struggle as the normal thing and with
resignation; but people who, when called upon to suffer
through their own and others' sins and follies, may be
capable of rising to heights of real goodness and noble
self-sacrifice."

Time has not been altogether unkind to De Marchi.
Since the end of World War II, a movie based on his
novel *Il cappello del prete* (London, 1935; *A Priest's Hat*)
and the recent publication of a handsome three-volume

edition of his literary production have been instrumental in encouraging the critics to revise earlier estimates of the writer. Regrettably, some readers have approached De Marchi with preconceived notions that have, in effect, made them unreceptive to a new assessment. Some have even complained that a minor figure such as De Marchi hardly deserves the attention he has been receiving. No responsible critic has, to my knowledge, denied the fact that De Marchi lacks the breadth of Manzoni, the vitality of Nievo, the originality of Verga, or the penetration of Svevo. What hopefully remains to be ascertained is just how we should see De Marchi, and the spot he may be said to occupy in his tradition. For surely, if we have systematically overrated Fogazzaro, it is likely that we may have been too demanding or severe toward the work of De Marchi. At best, he can be penetrating, introspective, and ironical. His chief quality is the compassion he felt for man's lot, and the tenderness with which he described human sufferings. He evokes, more than analyzes; he presents his tales in a suffused light that permits us to perceive how complex and baffling man can be. Action, in his novel, is always subordinate to his intention of dramatizing not what man does, but what he feels.

Emilio De Marchi was born in Milan on July 31, 1851, and died there fifty years later. He was raised by his mother, his father having died when Emilio was barely nine, attended the local schools, graduating first from the Liceo Beccaria and then from the Accademia Scientifica-Letteraria. All his life he aspired to recognition and esteem, both of which he achieved by hard work as secretary of his alma mater, as a teacher, journalist, critic, and writer. Although modest and retiring, he counted numerous friends in intellectual circles. Capuana, Verga, Fogazzaro, and Giacosa repeatedly praised his artistic and human gifts. His production was both varied and prolific: short shories, translations, poetry, criticism, and reportages. Most of it is justly forgotten; enough of it, on the other hand, has survived the crucial test of time to warrant our study.

Circumstances forced De Marchi to spend—or should one say consume?—an inordinate amount of time at his job, shut in an office and doing routine clerical work, "tied," as he once wrote Fogazzaro, "five hours a day, every day, to those filthy bureaucratic papers." Yet, without such an experience it is doubtful that he would have written the better part of his fiction which, as in the case of the later Italo Svevo, frequently deals with life in an office. While his penetrating eye enabled him to observe daily life and he accumulated a rich storehouse of memories from which he was to draw abundant material for his tales, his critical activity enabled him to think afresh the problems of the novel, and forced him to formulate certain views of literature that were to serve as the theoretical foundation of his narrative. For him, as he stated, "the artist must be the mirror of his time. He should strive to be honest and allow his own sensitivity to define his own temperament. Art cannot ask more than that." He strove to search for the "grave and solemn topics of life," yet he remained constantly aware of the ironies and paradoxes of existence. Similarly, while he acknowledged that "art that proposes to be too many things ends by being nothing," he entertained the implicit notion of artistic creation as an instrument to make people into better human beings—by making his readers aware of human shortcomings, he aimed at correcting them.

De Marchi lived in a dramatic period, during which his country was appreciating for the first time in her history the onerous responsibilities of freedom and was facing the vastly complex problems of political and social unification. In De Marchi's fiction, however, it is impossible to find the slightest hint of contemporary events. One gets the feeling of what life must have been like in Milan, toward the turn of the century, and what people must have been like in those years; but no attention is paid to their political ideas, or to their ideological stances. Ultimately, one must indeed conclude that De Marchi was infinitely fascinated by the puzzling, unpredictable character of man, who finds himself tangled in unmanageable situations, and not by the mysterious workings of history. He was preoccupied not with the bravery a few are able to display in moments of danger, but in the courage man must summon up every single day of his life. In a sense, he placed himself in the company of several writers—like Silvio Pellico, Massimo d'Azeglio, and Edmondo de Amicis—who, each in his own way, sought to depict a society not yet torn by conflicts, a society whose anguish could be redeemed or at least lessened only by a feeling of brotherhood, by a common awareness of the inescapable tragic implications of the human condition. De Marchi's routine activities seem to be fully consonant with his aspirations as a person. Whether he was editing the sheet called *La Buona Parola* (*The Kind Word*), teaching, or merely discharging what could only be envisioned as the modest clerical duties of the secretary of a distinguished academy, he always gave evidence of his desire to instill a sense of dignity, purpose, and responsibility into the minds of those who read him. Literature for him was never "a past-time for idlers, but an instrument to improve our life."

His most mature work, and the one that comes closest to giving us a complete statement about life, is *Demetrio Pianelli*, published in 1890. The novel is not only far more attractive than the earlier *The Priest's Hat* (the tale of a murdered priest, whose hat keeps reappearing on the scene and eventually drives a squandering baron to confess his horrible crime), but it is also closer to the artist's fundamentally melancholy attitude toward the cruelty of existence. As he had done in his previous novel, De Marchi charged a relatively simple story with great pathos and irony. But, while in *The Priest's Hat* he has used irony to bring the culprit to his punishment, dramatizing the fact that his crime had been unnecessary, in *Demetrio* its function is to show the gradual disenchantment with people and with life which turns the hero into a lonely man, hopelessly denied any opportunity to enjoy the smallest amount of happiness.

Protagonist of the novel is a simple office clerk Demetrio Pianelli. When his half-brother Cesarino commits suicide, after having appropriated a sizable amount of money from the bank that employs him, Demetrio decides to devote his energies and modest financial resources to helping the destitute little family get back on its feet. With time, however, Demetrio falls hopelessly in love with his sister-in-law Beatrice, a beautiful, demanding, but insensitive woman who fails to notice his affection and devotion, and who shows no appreciation for the numerous sacrifices he makes for her and her daughter. Placed in the awkward position of having to defend her reputation when one of his superiors makes advances to her, he is quickly and mercilessly punished: he is fined two months' salary and is transferred to a post in the Tuscan city of Grosseto, away from the few friends he has and from his family. Meanwhile, Beatrice marries Demetrio's cousin, Paolino, a wealthy farmer. The irony of their marriage is that Demetrio himself engineered the match, after realizing that Beatrice does not and cannot ever love him, so she will find in Paolino a fine husband and an excellent provider for her family.

The whole tale is suffused by a strain of resignation that gives the book its particular delicate melancholy. For the author, however, the resignation of his chief protagonist is hardly dictated by religious considerations, faith in a Divine Order, for instance, or confidence in God's Providence, but simply by the human awareness that often man must simply sacrifice himself so that others may be happy. De Marchi's merit consists not merely in recognizing a contemporary truth but in dramatizing it in an unusually low, restrained key, whose major strength is in the power of the understatements and simplicity of feelings. His style is limpid and objective, his attitude stern yet compassionate. The pages leading up to the suicide of Cesarino (called Lord Cosmetico by his friends because of the fastidiousness with which he dresses and grooms himself) are engrossing, and they strike us for their vigor and suspense. However despicable a character Cesarino is, he is also a figure whose humanity is perfectly comprehensible in the light of his egocentricity and shabby values.

De Marchi's artistic creativity is well evidenced in his

handling of the book's central character, Demetrio, a modest, retiring, somewhat selfish individual. In the hands of the author he becomes a man whose stature has immeasurably grown by the end of the novel, as he is forced by circumstances to accept a burden far heavier than he had ever anticipated. Demetrio's spirit of sacrifice, his patience and tolerance toward human beings is tested anew, and through this test he achieves a new human dimension. He gives of himself and of his resources generously and repeatedly, ultimately finding his strength in a love that is charity. He learns to give without expecting and much less asking any reward; he undoes his entire existence—his habits, his comfort, his security—in order that his sister-in-law and, above all, his small niece Arabella who grows fond of her uncle might find the security, stability, and affection not even Cesarino had been able to give them. Surprisingly enough, the numerous trials endured by Demetrio never make him a bitter, angry man—by giving of himself, he fulfills his destiny as a human being.

De Marchi's position in his own literature is perhaps clearer today than it was only a few years ago. It is impossible not to admire his work, for despite the fact that he lived in a historical era of turmoil and adjustment, in the midst of literary currents that could, and did, reach extreme positions, he remained steadfast in his purpose of finding and depicting in his fiction not the raw and savage aspects of man's character or the picturesque life in Italian hamlets. He sought to describe and illuminate the short-comings and frailties of the human temperament, but also the very qualities that in the last analysis redeem man and make him into something worthy of dignity and compassion. A writer from, and for, the middle class, De Marchi brought new force and meaning to the prosaic, humble everyday existence of the average individual; it is to his merit that he should have been able to dramatize, through tales of remarkable simplicity, that even the most modest life has its share of pathos and tragedy.

Once the power of our family came from Kings. . . . Now
it comes from the people. The difference is more in name
than in fact. Of course, it's not pleasant to depend on the
mob, but . . . history is monotonous repetition; men have
been, and will always be the same. Exterior conditions
change. Certainly there seems to be an abyss between Sicily
of 1860, still more or less feudal, and this of today, but the
difference is all on the surface. The first man to be elected
by a near-universal suffrage is not a member of the working-
class, or a bourgeois or a democrat; it is I, because I'm called
Prince of Francalanza. The prestige of the nobility is not
and cannot be extinguished.

These words, realistic to the point of bordering on
cynicism, are spoken by Prince Consalvo at the end of a
long novel titled *I vicerè* (New York, 1962; *The Viceroys*), and they certainly do justice to the spirit, if not to
the grand theme of the book. So engrossing is the tale the
novelist tells, and so ambivalent is his perspective, that
those who have immersed themselves in a careful reading
of the fantastic obsessions that are the very flesh of the
book have invariably reached vastly different conclusions
about its meaning. Some have taken the book as the
absorbing account of the struggle the already wealthy and
powerful Sicilian family of the Uzedas wages in order to
amass material possessions, gain additional political power
both at the local and national level, while at the same
time fighting to preserve the *status quo*. These readers

point to that, to carry its theme through, the story is purposely set in a milieu and in a time when the existing socio-political structure in Italy was rapidly collapsing, when the cries for reforms were loud, and restlessness great. Others have chosen to accept the book as a historical novel that intelligently dramatizes the meaning and implications of the events that brought unity and political independence to a formerly divided Italy. Still others have read it as a haunting study of the rivalries, petty jealousies, and secret schemings riddling a noble, decadent Sicilian family. The late Giuseppe Tomasi di Lampedusa, whose *Leopard* pivots on a similar theme as that of *The Viceroys*, disparagingly called the book "a picture of Sicilian aristocracy seen from the servants' hall," an obvious reference to the fact that it was written from the outside, as it were. Ultimately, while agreeing that in one sense or another, the novel may be all these and many more things, we shall have to acknowledge that its great theme is human egotism and pride, whose effects are minutely analyzed against the backdrop of an ideal betrayed. Betrayals, as we shall soon see, take place on different levels. Nonetheless, their constant presence on the scene suggests a hopeless conclusion about the sorry state of human relations, and indeed explains why the Prince should be so brutally candid in his final utterance, so contemptuous of the very people who have elected him to serve as their representative. The final point the novelist makes about the realities of power and politics may be disheartening, to be sure. On the other hand, the evidence he brings in support of a thesis developed throughout the book is both ample and persuasive: so long as people are what they are, they will always allow themselves to be exploited and manipulated by politicians eager to enlarge their already respectable empires.

The author of the extraordinary book, *The Viceroys*, was Federico De Roberto. He was born in Naples on January 16, 1861. At the age of ten, after his father (an army colonel in the service of the Bourbons) had passed away, he left Naples for his mother's birthplace, and thenceforth considered himself a native of Catania, where he completed his studies. Like many southern intellectuals, he spent a good part of his life in the North, especially in Florence and Milan, where he began his career as a writer, first as a contributor to various newspapers and periodicals, then as a literary critic and social observer, and finally as a novelist. In the cosmopolitan centers of the North he also became exposed to the literary theories and fiction stemming from France; there, too, he met the leading writers of his time—Verga, Capuana, Giacosa, and Praga among them—who befriended and encouraged him.

He lived through an era that alternated between hope and disillusionment, political freedom and political coercion, war and peace. He was born just a few weeks before the official unification of his nation was announced, lived under three different kings, and witnessed both the birth and death of democratic institutions when Mussolini's Blackshirts took over. He was a prolific writer indeed, the author of some thirty books of criticism, short stories, pseudo-scientific treatises, as well as several novels. None of these works, however, compels the attention of the contemporary reader as much as *The Viceroys*, "whose real protagonist," as Mr. Colquhoun aptly points out in his introduction to the English translation of the book, "is the Year of Unification, *dies irae*, 1860 itself." In this respect, the novel has something in common with such recent works as Italo Calvino's *La giornata di uno scrutatore* (*A Day of a Voting Poll's Inspector*) and Guglielmo Petroni's *Il colore della terra* (*The Color of the Earth*), in that they depict the mood of a nation whose hopes have been dashed by the inevitable political and moral compromises that follow a great historical crisis.

De Roberto actually began his literary career at a moment when the creative arts were experiencing a phase of unusual restlessness in his native country. The poets who had commanded the esteem of the previous generation, from Giovanni Prati and Aleardo Aleardi to the epigones of Manzoni and Romanticism, were suddenly dethroned and turned into objects of ridicule. Verismo, whose tenets of objectivity and realism had been boldly proclaimed by Capuana and Verga, had already experienced with the publication of I Malavoglia and Mastro-don Gesualdo what in retrospect was to be recognized as its finest hour. A score of other prolific writers, among whom were Capuana, Serao, Di Giacomo, and, later on, Grazia Deledda, continued to compose novels that focussed on the life in their respective native provinces; at times, as in the case of Capuana, the regionalistic setting lost its importance to psychological probings. From beyond the Alps, Darwin's 1859 findings on the Origin of Species, Taine's theory of la race, le moment et le milieu, and the doctrinaire programs of Emile Zola, were permeating the intellectual climate in Italy. We must therefore look to De Roberto's sympathies for the critical postures of his friends Capuana and Verga, and to his interest in the psychological and pseudoscientific trends of French fiction in the second half of the nineteenth century, if we are to single out the intellectual fathers of our novelist. Thus, in setting, style and themes, his first book, La sorte (Fate), 1887, is clearly modeled on Verga's tales, while in his second book, Processi verbali (Verbal Trials), 1890, one senses the presence of Zola, a writer De Roberto would, in later years, alternately repudiate and imitate. In Ermanno Roeli and L'albero della scienza (The Tree of Science), brought out in 1889 and 1890 respectively, one notices a progressive movement toward the impersonality of Gustave Flaubert and the psychological interest of Paul Bourget.

Despite his early allegiance to the principles of realism (scrupulous observation, sincerity of expression, impersonality of narration had been the main tenets of his poetics) De Roberto became gradually disenchanted by its limitations. For some years, he found himself torn between the idea of following the path traced by Verga or that of Bourget, who seemed to him a writer anticipating the general direction in which the novel would move in future years. In this sense, De Roberto actually lived the dilemmas and uncertainties of a writer who found himself in a transitional period. While in his early years he had implicitly approved of what may be called the compartmentalization of knowledge as an effective and efficient way to deal with human experience, he became gradually aware of the inadequacies of a method that confined itself to dealing with man's external reality, rather than with his psychology, which was sure to hold the key to an ultimate understanding of human behavior. In a number of critical and creative works, he elaborated his position. He stressed the artistic necessity of concentrating not only on what is healthy about man, but on his degenerate, morally and physically corrupt sides; he denied the validity of such important tenets as impersonality of narrative and objectivity of point of view, and claimed that "one cannot analyze situations and characters without sympathizing with them," thus assuming a stance diametrically opposite to the one he had formerly held. Along with other writers, De Roberto perceived that *verismo* had taken the writer as far as it could. Unfortunately, the wretchedness of life in the provinces, the drama of the exploited, miserable peasants, and the powerful theme of property—Verga's *la roba*—had been overplayed, if not overstated. A greater effort had to be made by the artist so that economics, psychology, history, and the sciences be fully utilized in order to explore more profoundly, and arrive at sounder conclusions about, man's lot.

What persuaded De Roberto to abandon the relatively simple world of his early fiction, a world largely made up of peasants with primitive instincts and basic longings, for the more complicated bourgeois and aristocratic characters of his mature novels? Perhaps he grew tired of dealing with opposite dualisms (life in the provinces versus life in the urban centers, primitive characters versus sophisticated ones, and so forth), or perhaps he became aware of the fact that he had never been interested in the preoccupations and life of the peasants, and therefore felt alien to them. However that may be, he must have felt a special challenge in the possibility of explaining the failures of his early heroes in terms of historical circumstances, heredity, and flaw of character. Possibly too, he wished to dramatize two dominating traits of the human personality more consistently found in sophisticated sensibilities: a drive aimed at self-destruction, on the one hand, and a pervasive, idyllic, if vaguely understood yearning to achieve happiness, on the other.

L'illusione (*The Illusion*), the second of a cycle of three novels De Roberto was to write, was actually conceived and published first. One critic has called it, with some justification I think, De Roberto's attempt to reconcile naturalism with psychology, so as to produce a book that would have the scientific character of an experiment and the insight of a work of fiction capable of probing the human psyche. As it turned out, *The Illusion* proved to be the least successful and convincing volume of the saga of the Uzedas. What is interesting, at least from the historical point of view, is that while writing it, the author conceived his three-volume cycle and visualized *The Illusion* as a sequel to *The Viceroys*, whose story would be carried over into a final book, *L'imperio* (*The Empire*). To give the scheme a structural unity, he planned to concentrate on a single family, rather than aiming—after Balzac—at a sweeping portrayal of nineteenth-century Italian society. Through the events of a limited number of characters, drawn mainly from the upper and middle classes, De Roberto aimed at fashioning a work that was patterned, in theme if not always in structure, after such disparate novels as Rovani's *Cento anni* (*One Hundred Years*), Manzoni's *The Betrothed* (characterized by the critic De Sanctis as a successful fusion of the historical and the psychological novel), and Zola's *Les Rougon-Macquarts*.

The Illusion is frankly a *roman à thèse*: by the time we reach the end of the first of the book, with its fine chapters describing the mistaken upbringing of the heroine, Teresa Uzedi Duffredi di Casaura, we are beginning to feel impatient with the story, annoyed by the author's overly deterministic outlook, and by the heavy-handed way in which he tries to demonstrate *ad nauseam* the irreparable damage environment and early training have done to Teresa's character. And if it is true that De Roberto has an unusual ability to make his characters supremely self-aware, he also dooms them to a common fate of defeat generated now by their selfishness, now by their greedy ambition, now by their upbringing. At the bottom of it all, there is an implicit moral: a society that neither predicates, nor lives up to, a sound system of moral values inevitably dedicates itself to perpetuating false ideas about the meaning of life and man's condition that can only lead to a destruction of the body and the soul, a hopeless waste of human resources and potentialities. Unfortunately, everything in the novel seems almost contrived to substantiate the thesis offered, and the result is an insistence that becomes repetitiousness in many of the episodes and monotony in the treatment of a score of characters that are one-dimensional, cold, and mechanical. De Roberto is at his best when he takes us into the intimate life and doings of Sicilian aristocracy, describing its parties and festivities, its futile talk, its mundane ambitions, and many of its vulgar conventions. "It is a strong novel, even if it is a bitter one, which depresses [rather than] fortifies [the reader]," commented the novelist Antonio Fogazzaro. It is a judgment we have no difficulty accepting today, as we read the work with greater perspective.

"Between *The Illusion* and *The Viceroys*," writes Gianni Grama, "the 'psychological' and the 'historical' novel, there is a material and qualitative difference in structure and tone, in language and style, in depth and narrative breadth." The remark is to the point, and the scope and dimension of *The Viceroys* were to remain unequaled by anything else De Roberto wrote during his prolific career.

It is instructive to place the novel side-by-side with another notable narrative of a similar type, Nievo's *The Castle of Fratta*, to appreciate the qualities that lend *The Viceroys* its undeniable uniqueness. The first thing that is bound to strike us is the tone of the novel, seldom reflective and never gentle, even when the events described are charged with considerable pain or sorrow, but usually caustic, almost derisive. Nievo's book, as we have noted, is imbued with a nostalgia for a world that is no more; yet, it remains open-minded and even generous toward the new era, ready to accept it—not to fight it, partly because changes are inevitable in human affairs, and partly because such changes may well bring greater fulfillment and happiness to the Italian nation. None of this is true in *The Viceroys*: the sting of the fraud perpetrated by its protagonists is too painful to allow either the novelist or his reader to forget that if we have witnessed the collapse of an old world, we must realize that the so-called new order is but a promulgation, in different dress, of the injustices and the inequalities of the old. Finally, Nievo masterfully fuses his narrative about a tumultuous historical period with the story of a passionate, obstinate, and tender love between the two heroes. By contrast, De Roberto, while remaining faithful to his intention of giving us a partially accurate account of the history of Sicily between 1855 and 1882, interweaves the story, told with fine attention to every detail of the psychology of its characters, with the hatreds of a bizarre family. The subject of De Roberto's book dictates its somber, gloomy colors, the cheerless quality of much of its action (one thinks here of the expectations of Nievo's Carlino, of his dash and courage and, above all, of his integrity), and the degrading life it depicts.

Both in its goal and technique, *The Viceroys*, while it has several common links with De Roberto's previous novels, differs rather drastically from the book that was to constitute its sequel. In *The Illusion*, in fact, the novelist had sought to describe the fiber of certain social strata through a careful study of a restricted number of personages. By contrast, *The Viceroys* is substantially more ambitious both in terms of chronological treatment and of character study. Moreover, the society it scrutinizes is temperamentally and intellectually more varied. Fundamentally, unlike *The Illusion*, the novel does not propose to be a mere chronicle of the Uzedas, whose internal feuds and involvement in political affairs become a matter of common concern, since their actions have a profound and disturbing effect upon history. The intention of the novel is to provide us with an interpretative analysis, reached by a writer uninvolved in the story itself, of certain historical events that shaped the course of Italian life in the South for several decades, giving us at the same time a study in depth of the origins, motivations, and results of human passions.

The story is set in Sicily, and spans about a quarter of a century. At the center of the stage stands the Uzeda family (descendants of the Spanish Viceroys who ruled the island), composed of Donna Teresa's seven children. The oldest, Donna Angiolina, has been sent to a convent, as was traditional with many families when the first child was a girl, and she is now Sister Maria of the Cross, Nun of San Placido. Then come her three sons, Don Giacomo XIV, Prince of Francalanza, married first to Margherita Grazzeri and then to Donna Graziella Carvano (his children are Consalvo, Prince of Mirabella, and Teresa, later Duchess Radalí and the heroine of *The Illusion*). Next in line is Don Lodovico, Prior of San Nicola, later elected Cardinal; then there is Don Raimondo, Count of Lumera, married first to Donna Matilde and then to Donna Isabella Fersa. The fifth child is Donna Chiara, Marchioness of Villardita (who is married to Federico, Marquis of Villardita); the sixth child is Don Ferdinando, of Pietra dell'Ovo, and, finally, Donna Lucrezia, later married to Benedetto Giulente. The impressive cast is completed by Donna Teresa's brothers and sister-in-law: Don Gaspare, Duke of Oragua; Don Blasco, a Benedictine monk; Cavaliere Don Eugenio and Donna Ferdinanda.

These, however, are only the main characters of a novel extraordinarily rich in personages; their lives and destinies are followed by the author with the utmost scrupulousness as he takes us into the intimacy of family discussions, as well as into more distant contacts with the large staff of servants, tenant farmers, tailors, and various artisans who take care of the family's needs. Later in the book, as the story turns toward a closer interaction between the people and the Uzedas (an interaction made necessary by the changing political climate rather than by personal choice) the crowds come more directly into the picture. De Roberto's treatment of them is similar to Manzoni's; like the great Milanese novelist, De Roberto also seems to consider the masses as herds of sheep, led blindfolded by men with stronger will to a destiny not clearly comprehended.

The treatment of the story is strictly chronological, and in every other way the novel is structurally traditional. As in most historical narratives, we follow the fortune and fate of the various characters from the omniscient point of view of the author in a manner that is both orderly and exhaustive. But, unlike Manzoni's *The Betrothed*, the author never feels the necessity of supplementing the facts given in the story with additional information gathered through excursions to libraries in search of old records or dusty scholarly tomes that might extend our knowledge of the period in question. The facts speak eloquently for themselves, principally because the story has a contemporary setting: indeed, many of its characters were closely patterned after people who had really lived, a fact that impelled Luigi Capuana to request the key that would permit him to identify accurately the various prominent figures of the novel.

Because *The Viceroys* is a historical novel as well as a novel about politics, each of its three parts ends with an event of first magnitude: Part One ends with the defeat of the Kingdom of the Two Sicilies and its unification with Italy; Part Two ends with the conquest of Rome in 1870; Part Three ends with the broadening of election laws. Each part is in turn accompanied by a political victory for one of the Uzedas: first, the election of Don Gaspare to the Parliament, then the political success of Don Blasco, who masterminds a highly profitable purchase of ecclesiastical property; finally, the election of Prince Consalvo to the House, while his uncle is assured of a Senate seat.

Both the past and the present are kept constantly before us: the former, by the numerous discussions of the family's nobility typically illustrated by the *Sicilian Herald,* the work to which Don Eugenio devotes (or should one say squanders?) most of his existence and whose publication eventually bankrupts him; by the reading of the will of Donna Teresa; and by Donna Ferdinanda's perusal of the account of the family's past in the *Genealogical Theater* of Sicily, where no less than thirty large pages are devoted to the Uzedas.

The book opens with what must be regarded as a symbolic death scene, which points to the fact that, among other things, the novel is a story about death. Not death in the ordinary sense, however, even if in the course of the novel we witness many of its characters disappear from the world of the living—invariably struck by hideous diseases—but the death of an era, of a way of life, of certain social and moral values, as well as lofty political ideals. It is fitting, therefore, that Donna Teresa Uzeda and Risà, Princess of Francalanza, should be the first to die, and cause havoc among her surviving family and servants. Her work is done, her mission accomplished. A despotic, powerful, shrewd, and ambitious woman, she has spent the better part of her life setting the affairs of her family in order, driven to the edge of bankruptcy by the incompetence of her stupid spouse, long dead. She has carefully raised her offspring, less with the affection of a mother than with the coldness of an intriguer, planning their lives with infinite care, favoring only the children who have the potentials of true leaders, and thus fomenting a rivalry amongst them that will make their existence as adults even more wretched. The calculations of the Princess, unfortunately, have not taken into proper account the unpredictability of nature itself. She has patiently built an edifice that, however solid and admirable its architecture may seem to the outsider, is doomed to crumble, if only in the distant future, because it has been built upon the shifting sands of egotism and the mire of hatred. Whatever good instinct was present in the sensibility of her seven children when they were young has been repressed and destroyed. Hunger for power, thirst for wealth are accompanied by an equally haunting fear of death through madness or hereditary diseases. "Everyone," writes Vittorio Spinazzola, "must be ready to sacrifice himself; implacable priests of a ferocious divinity, the Uzedas devote the best part of their personality to the pride of nobility, destroying the future of their children, resorting to lying, cheating, and to the filthiest baseness."

A profound dissension, springing from jealousy and rivalry, and a continual conflict with society are the two sources of tension in the novel. Even though torn by personal strife, the Uzedas are capable of being magnificently united in acknowledging, respecting, and fostering the concept of superiority of their race, and the fame and respect it has either earned or conquered through wealth and power. The course of the life of each of the children has been charted with an eye turned not toward self-fulfillment but to the preservation of the family's glory and prestige. The whole book reads like a case study of how through manipulation, persuasion, threat, and deceit the lives of Donna Teresa's seven children, and those of her husband's brothers and sister, have been bent to fill a place in a preestablished design. Don Blasco and his nephew Don Lodovico, for instance, are forced into religious life simply to keep the family patrimony intact for the older children. Don Gaspare, Don Eugenio, Ferdinando, and Donna Ferdinanda are left to their own resources to rise out of their condition. Not all fare well, by any means: Don Eugenio actually dies a beggar, while Don Gaspare, who has an uncanny ability to move with the changing political winds, enjoys enormous success. It goes almost without saying that he is not interested in politics as a public service. Elected deputy and sent by his constituents to Turin, he reaps tangible financial harvests from information on the political situation, available to him as a lawmaker. His motto is modeled on Cavour's with a wonderfully apt modification: "Now that Italy is made, let us tend to our [*personal*] affairs." He gambles on the Stock Exchange, founds the Credit Bank in his native Catania, makes free and illegal use of public funds, and ends up a truly powerful and consequential figure. When the voting laws are changed, in 1882, he sees his own political position threatened. He loses no time in making a Machiavellian deal with his opponents and is elected to the Senate, while his clever nephew Consalvo begins waging a rough, but skillfully planned, political battle that will eventually see him elected to the House of Parliament.

Others are less successful: Ferdinando, for example, dies haunted by his persecution complex, his fear of death, and his gnawing worry that his own family is trying to cheat him out of his share of the inheritance that he has all but squandered. Donna Ferdinanda, despite her enormous success as a usurer, leads an acrimonious, empty existence.

The hunger for power, money, and status drives all the Uzedas alike. Don Blasco does not let the fact that he has joined a monastic order stand in his way and curtail his ambition to reach goals that are identical to those of his mercenary, greedy family. When his life of debauchery is threatened by political changes, he is quick to curse the northern liberals, Cavour, Garibaldi, the King himself, and all those who are endangering the *status quo*. Then the new government, through a money-making edict, decides to proceed with the sale of confiscated ecclesiastical property, he extracts profitable information from Don Gaspare, purchases a piece of valuable property for a pittance, and even becomes a vociferous anticlerical who expresses his hope that the Pope will be brought down to his knees by the national government.

By the same token Benedetto Giulente, the son of a well-to-do bourgeois and a passionate advocate of liberal causes, is not immune from the devastating and immoral compromises that make politics a filthy game. He takes an active part in Garibaldi's bold landing on the island, fights valiantly as one of his troops, is wounded during the battle on the Volturno river, and naïvely thinks "himself destined to guide the Uzeda heir [Consalvo] in public life for a long time." His awakening comes swiftly and rudely, for in the administrative elections he is tenth on the list of candidates. His political career comes to an abrupt end when he finally understands that he is but a pawn in the hands of Don Gaspare and Consalvo: "You're all the same!" he exclaims in supreme disgust, "a bunch of arrogant scoundrels!" His reaction is comprehensible and eminently justified, but it has taken him far too long to understand what makes the special world of the Uzedas go round. By comparison Consalvo is a real professional in the rules of the game. Even in his youth, "he had no belief in the sincerity of other people's faith either. Monarchy or republic, religion or atheism, for him they all just depended on material or moral advantage, immediate or future. . . . So to him there was nothing apart from self-interest, and to satisfy his self-love he was ready to pursue every means at hand." This is a reasonably accurate summing-up of how Consalvo looks at the world.

The character of the young Prince, destined to be one of the dominating figures on the political scene of modern Italy (apparently modeled on Antonio Paterno Castello, Marquis of Saint Giuliano and Minister of Foreign Affairs between 1910–14), is carefully drawn in the book, and no biographical detail relevant to our understanding of his complex personality is missing. We see him proud and sure of himself when still a boy; we follow his education, his travels, his bitter feuds with his sickly father, his foresight in recognizing that the new political era which his country is entering will require a different brand of politician. He studies his own nation and its people, he broadens his views by visiting other countries, he mingles with politicians and kingpins, careful not to offend anyone, while cultivating the respect of everyone. His career really begins only after his father's death, but its trajectory is meteoric. The final section of the book deals almost exclusively with the fashion in which his education, his willpower, and his astuteness begin paying dividends. Yet, for all the success that awaits him, he, too, is no happy man. The thought of death from one of the horrible diseases to which the Uzedas seem to be especially prone, and the corruption flowing in the blood of his family— after centuries of intermarriages and dissipated living— haunt him.

> Consalvo . . . was thinking with terror of his fearful disease which would one day gnaw away and destroy his own body at that moment so full of life. The impoverished blood of the ancient race was making, after Ferdinando, another premature victim, for his father was scarcely fifty-five years old. Would he too die before his time, before achieving his triumph, killed by those terrible ills which struck down the Uzedas while they were still young? His father would have given all his riches to live a year, a month, a day longer. What would he himself give for the vivid healthy blood of a peasant to flow in his own veins? . . . "Nothing!"

Consalvo enjoys his victories, even if he is aware that "All must be paid for!" Somehow, at times he even believes that the destiny that has befallen the other members of his family will spare him: "He had no fear of falling into the Uzeda madness: all he had inherited from his family were its riches and its power. And this depiction of justice by him was another reason for self-congratulation." He promptly resigns the position of mayor that has been marred by fiscal irresponsibility and corruption, and fills the vacuum created by Don Gaspare's decision to run for the Senate by preparing himself to occupy a seat in the Parliament. Indeed, the last pages of the novel read like a miniature study of the making of a deputy and of the magical transformation he undergoes in order to please friends and placate enemies. All along, while professing to have the people's best interests at heart and claiming that he is committed to work for their welfare, "he felt an infinite contempt for the mob, and a violent rancor against whoever tried to bar his way." Much like his Uncle Raimondo, he is a forerunner *sui generis* of the hero of D'Annunzio, the prototype of the superman whose primary concern is the satisfaction of his own ego, the fulfillment of his ambitions and pleasures.

He has also something of Stendhal's Jean Sorel and de Maupassant's Bel-Ami.

All the Uzedas share a common revulsion toward people, and for them, as in the case of Consalvo, "direct contact with things or people was a torture." Such distaste for communion is yet another manifestation of the contempt the Uzedas feel for the masses, and of their own special fear that such contacts will actually hasten, or intensify, the physical degeneration that haunts them day and night. All the principal characters of *The Viceroys* are treated in a similar way, all more or less evil, all driven by fanatical obsessions, all painted with colors whose darkness makes the tableau all the more somber and monotonous to the eye than it need have been. There is really no positive character in this tale that may serve as suitable contrast to the corruption, materialism, and greed that runs deep in the blood of the Uzedas. There is not, nor can there be, any intervention of Divine Providence, for in the world of De Roberto religion is a mockery, both useless and irrelevant in terms of enabling the Uzedas to achieve their ambitious goals. His fantasy fabricates a life where the coarsest aspirations, the basest ambitions, and the most sinister machinations have free reign. "The power of the novel," writes Spinazzola, "is precisely in the exasperating pessimism pervading the representation of a world where pure and sincere feelings have no opportunity to manifest themselves; and, [to the reader] De Roberto will seem the poet of a sorrow that can neither be resigned nor consoled." *The Viceroys* is a novel of passions, not of tears; of violence, not of love, lest it be sexual; it is a disconcerting but true-to-life tale of the meaning, the uses, and misuses of power in periods of political turmoil.

In the preceding pages it has been noted that *The Viceroys* is a novel of customs and manners, a superb family portrait, and an illuminating, if partial, narrative concerning a pivotal historical period. In this sense, De Roberto may easily be called the writer who, in Italy, carried the novel as far as the assumptions of realism and naturalism would permit. The notable sides of the novel are many. From the point of view of content, certainly its fast-moving episodes and its feminine studies, done with the subtlety of an artist and the knowledge of a man obviously familiar with the scientific side of psychology; from the point of view of structure, the division of the book into parts that correspond to different historical periods is an interesting innovation in an otherwise conventional narrative pattern. Finally, from the linguistic angle, *The Viceroys* is particularly original for its rich diversity of diction. De Roberto's language spans all the way from the solemn to the mocking, from the serious to the ironic, from the pompousness of the aristocracy to the racy colloquialisms of the Sicilian plebe.

The stylistic variety is matched by traces of numerous influences that may well make *The Viceroys* a rewarding study for future writers of dissertations. There is enough in the book to satisfy all tastes: from a Manzonian penchant for historical-psychological biographies in miniature to Verga's pervasive concern with the economic factor as the overriding element determining man's fate; from the psychological approach of Capuana and Bourget to the scientific one of Zola and the regional one of the school of *verismo*. Whatever his flaws—which range from occasional clumsiness to repetitiousness, from an occasional lack of restraint to an overly deterministic view—at his best De Roberto is capable of the grand sweep of Balzac, the stylistic clarity of Flaubert and of an obsession with sickness and degeneracy sure to remind us of Zola and the Goncourt brothers.

If a good part of De Roberto's literary production seems dated and mechanical, *The Viceroys* has lost little of its relevance for the reader of today as a valid depiction of human folly and pride. Indeed, the ironical undertone of the entire novel has a distinctive contemporary flavor: men, De Roberto claims, are basically corrupt and generally unchangeable. Even when the curtain goes up and a new era is ushered in, there are those ready to exploit the passions of the past for the selfish interests of today and tomorrow. People are always the same, even if the garbs they put on as befits the occasion readily mislead the onlookers into thinking that the fat barons and exploiters of yesteryear have suddenly, almost magically, turned into the wise, charitable and foresighted leaders of today. Readers of De Roberto, from the conservative Croce to the Marxist critics, have taken issue with such a pessimistic and, perhaps, unfair view. No one, on the other hand, has denied that so persuaded De Roberto was of his truth that he decided to devote himself to creating what was to turn out to be a remarkable picture of a society bent upon walking on the masses and their simplest aspirations so as to retain its precious power. For all the passing of time, such a picture remains unforgettable; and long after finishing the book, the reader will be haunted by the many notable episodes that make De Roberto's tale a true tour de force; the frenzy, the bickerings, and the cold intrigues depicted have a brilliancy bordering on hallucination, with a strange surrealistic quality about them. *The Viceroys* is truly, in Mr. Colquhoun's definition, "a gigantic novel: cool, resourceful and imaginative."

De Roberto's ambition to present the drama of the great confrontation between the South and the new Kingdom of Italy possibly inspired Luigi Pirandello's *I vecchi e i giovani* (*The Old and the Young*), a novel that depicts a similar socio-political conflict between the old and the young generations at the turn of the century. But if the Italian and international audience reads De Roberto today, having rediscovered him several decades after his death in 1927, it is less for the influence he exerted upon other writers (notably on the late Vitaliano Brancati and Francesco Jovine, both Sicilians), pervasive as it might have been. It is simply, I suggest, because his books, along with those of his contemporaries Verga, Capuana, and Serao among them, mirror the past blunders of a society culturally advanced and socially in the retrograde. For all the flaws that mar *The Viceroys*, the book remains today, seventy years after its publication, a candid, absorbing reflection of an era that saw two drastically diverse cultures join and begin the long metamorphosis toward fusion. As such, and as a half-imagined and half-real interpretation of a nation's first steps toward real unity, *The Viceroys* will remain, for years to come, a prime document necessary to understand the elusive character of the Italian people.

6   THE TRAGIC WORLD OF
VERGA'S PRIMITIVES

AFTER ALESSANDRO MANZONI, it is Giovanni Verga who is accorded the honored second place in modern Italian fiction. Dubbed by the critics "the greatest novelist Italy has produced after Manzoni," Verga has long been consigned to the group of classical writers who enjoy the dismal fate of being frequently mentioned, rarely understood, and almost never closely read, except by the happy few. Ever since the publication, in 1919, of Luigi Russo's ground-breaking work that put Verga's achievement and importance in proper perspective, many monographs and countless articles on him have made their appearance. By and large, however, a positive critical estimate has done little to change the taste of the large reading public, for which the stark, tragic world of Verga's better novels has held far less fascination than that of his lesser, conventional, and trivial works, such as *Tigre reale* (*Royal Tigress*) and *Eros*. Only in recent months was this deplorable trend suddenly and inexplicably reversed. An edition of almost 200,000 paperback copies of *I Malavoglia* (New York, 1964; *The House by the Medlar Tree*) and another edition of *Mastro-don Gesualdo* (New York, 1955) were sold out in less than a fortnight.

From many angles, Verga's figure looms large on the literary scene of modern Italy. The magnitude and meaning of his lesson, the significance of his presence in the world of the novel can be perceived only through the practice of the novelists who have emerged in the last two decades. The objectivity he recommended and practiced during the most important phase of his career, the difficult operation he performed on the aulic, literary language of his country, his deep compassion for the plight of a suffering humanity, his vision of a society whose structure, drives, and goals can largely be measured by irresistible economic laws and by a persistent human hunger for material improvement, constitute but a small part of the rich legacy of ideas, insights, and technical-linguistic innovations he brought to the art of the novel. For the writers who have followed him, the problems of life and literature that concerned him persist in haunting their imagination.

Giovanni Verga was born in Catania in 1840. He was educated first at the private school of Antonino Abate, and then at the University of Catania. During the better part of his productive years he traveled extensively, living in such exciting cultural centers as Florence and Milan, where he made many friends among writers and critics. Personally and intellectually, Verga led a life immersed in the doings of his era. Yet, he founded no school, had no disciples and, although he did commit his artistic credo to the printed page, he never permitted himself to become embroiled in literary controversies.

By comparison with many writers, Verga's career spans a rather extended period of time; his first work was published in 1861, his last one, in 1902. Nonetheless, the best of his fiction—consisting of a respectable number of short stories and two novels—was produced within a single decade, 1878–88. After that, although he remained active, publishing numerous stories, novels, and a handful of undistinguished plays, he lived in a state of semiretirement. In 1893 he left Milan, where he had resided for several years, abandoned the cultural circles in which he had assiduously participated, and withdrew to his native city. There he spent the remaining years of his life meditating on his past experiences, planning the continuation of a five-novel cycle that never went beyond the first chapter of the third book, and simply watching the world go by. In 1920 the Italian Government honored him by naming him Senator; two years later he died.

There are at least two sides of Verga's personality that must be considered in a study of his work, and so strikingly do they differ that it is hard to conceive that they were parts of a man who could write, on the one hand, such a novel as *Una peccatrice* (*A Sinner*), 1866, and, on the other, *The House by the Medlar Tree*. Indeed, one is tempted to say that Verga had not one but two different careers, each with its own zenith and declining stage. First, of course, there is the youthful production, consisting of several historical novels Verga composed when he was still an adolescent or a law student at the university, the unpublished "Amore e patria" ("Love and Motherland"), *I Carbonari della Montagna*, 1861, and *Sulle laguna* (*On the Lagunas*), 1863. These works were followed by a number of novels in the romantic tradition, mostly stories of illicit or sensual love, composed during his sojourns in Florence and Milan. Such books, written during the first decade and a half of his literary career, present a world that only seemingly bears little or no relation with his other world, the grim, deterministic, harsh world of *la roba* in *The House by the Medlar Tree*, and *Mastro-don Gesualdo*. Actually, everything Verga wrote seems to be characterized by the same pessimism, the same frustrated yearning for happiness and well-being, the same tragic fate to which most, if indeed not all, of his characters are doomed.

As a rule, his early heroes are drawn from the aristocracy and the middle class. They are pseudo-intellectuals, would-be artists, spineless human beings Verga must have studied at close rage when he frequented the fashionable salons of Mesdames Ciaffei and Greppi. Generally speaking, the typical hero of the early Verga is always falling in love with a woman older than himself, invariably attracted by her magnetic personality and power of seduction. The attraction, at first seemingly innocent, becomes a sentimental tie and soon blossoms into a full-fledged love affair, complete with the inevitable sexual fulfillment and the equally inevitable boredom that follows the consummation of such love. At times, the relationship proves to be too much for one of the lovers, one of whom (usually the heroine) dies of tuberculosis or of a mysterious malady; less frequently we have a suicide. The plot is standard, and the technique shows little diversity from one novel to the other. Characters and events change to be sure, but after a while they become practically indistinguishable from the personages and events of the previous books. The feminine characters seem to be regularly stronger than the heroes, and certainly appear to know what they want out of life and how they intend to achieve their objectives. Their major weapon is their voluptuousness, which they use effectively to trap and enslave their unsophisticated suitors.

In *Storia di una capinera* (*Story of a Linnet*), 1870, for example, we find a young novice falling in love with a young man who eventually marries her stepsister. The heroine joins a religious order, but unable to cope with her disappointment and frustration, succumbs to madness and dies. *A Sinner* revolves around the love nourished by a law student by the name of Pietro Busio for the attractive Narcisa Valderi Countess of Prato. The heroine first rejects her suitor, then falls in love with him—by this time Pietro has become a famous playwright and poet—only to become aware that their relationship is rapidly becoming meaningless. She then takes her life, while Pietro, wishing to forget the past, withdraws to a small provincial town and earns his bread by composing occasional poetry. *Royal Tigress* is only slightly different from the pattern, as it is modeled on the traditional love triangle. Here we have Giorgio La Ferlita, a weakling, who falls in love with Nata, a wealthy Russian incurably ill with tuberculosis. Before returning to her motherland with her husband, Nata promises Giorgio that she will return to Italy to die. She does indeed return, only to discover that during her absence Giorgio has married and is now a father. Upon learning of Nata's return, Giorgio rushes to her and at last their love is consummated. Nata's death and the hero's realization that the world will not be the same provide a fitting conclusion to the story. Not much different is the case of *Eva*, 1873, justly called the best and most typical of Verga's minor works. Here we have the hero, an aspiring painter by the name of Enrico Lanti, falling in love with a dancer, Eva, who leads a carefree, amoral existence. His love is returned for a while; but eventually, the two decide to part. One day Enrico, who has become a famous artist, asks Eva to return to live with him. To attain his wish, he even challenges Eva's lover to a duel, but his attempts to reconquer her heart fail miserably. He then goes back to his native town, where he dies of consumption amidst depressingly abject conditions.

It would be interesting to pursue further a study of Verga's early novels, but it is doubtful whether it would produce any startling discovery. Ultimately, we must simply admit that his first literary efforts were franky autobiographical, and their interest is limited to a disclosure of the books the author himself must have been reading in that period, the life he was leading, the people who befriended him, and the places in which he lived. What one invariably finds striking about the early heroes of Verga is their incredible mediocrity, their inability to react to anything that is not a sensual desire. They are weak, immoral, empty; they neither hold any values, nor are they restrained or inspired by religious, civil, or intellectual beliefs. They move in a world that is the civilized world of Verga himself, a world of inane talk, trite events, ridiculous passions, exaggerated mannerisms, immature behavior. It is also a world where people do not work to earn their bread, seem to fear nothing except their eventual sexual desiccation, and engage in such diversions as travel less because this is what they *want* to do than because this is the *thing* to do, the fashionable element that provides distraction and a mild degree of amusement to an otherwise empty, boring, shabby existence.

The year 1874, barely a few months before the completion of *Eros*, marks an important turning point in Verga's career, for it signals the beginning of his second moment of creativity. It was in that year that the Sicilian composed "Nedda: A Sicilian Sketch." It is in this brief work of barely twenty pages that we find the first concrete evidence that something in the creative spirit of Verga was prodding him to return to a world he knew so well in the depth of his subconsciousness. Strikingly different from anything the novelist had written up to that time, the *bozzetto* does not yet represent a complete, sharp break with his earlier work. It may be compared to a new, tenuously stated theme that appears for the first time in a musical composition to be realized fully and satisfactorily only in a subsequent opus. In other words, "Nedda" is the first concrete evidence of Verga's realization that his earlier narrative had largely dealt with an acquired experience, not one necessarily close to the center of his sensibility. If his Florentine and Milanese experiences had been invaluable to him in enabling him to become socially and intellectually known and accepted, they had not revealed what his commitments as an artist should be, or how he might legitimately renew the genre he had chosen for himself.

From the purely stylistic point of view, "Nedda" is easily classifiable as a story in the tradition of clear, unpretentious short narratives. Thematically the story does represent a bold break with the previous novels. Gone are the bejeweled women, the aspiring intellectuals, the affluent northern bourgeois life, the decadent passions of the flesh. In "Nedda" we find ourselves suddenly thrust into the world of the peasants exploited by the rich landowners, infinitely oppressed by what Verga's world view will ultimately recognize as one of mankind's greatest evils: poverty. We smell not the delicious perfumes of the ladies, but the pungent odor of onions, black bread and minestra; we see not the delicate, elegant, and alluring gowns but the dirty, miserable rags of the olive pickers. We are placed not in the busy, hurried cities of the north, but in the hard landscape of the island of Sicily. We have no time to know either pleasure or boredom, only pain and work. The greatest human joy is experienced when people can find work and earn enough money to overcome the immediate needs of food and shelter.

The short tale recounts the story of three deaths, all perhaps avoidable in a different social order, and of the loneliness and hopelessness of the poor. Nedda's mother, gravely ill and unable to receive adequate medical attention, dies, leaving her daughter alone in the world. Her only relative, Zio Giovanni, is too selfish to care either about her well-being or her fate. Nedda is proud to earn her own bread working on a farm; there she meets and falls in love with Janu, a young man who, like Nedda, is an olive picker. Out of their brief, intense love, a baby is born. One day Janu, ill with malaria, falls from an olive tree and dies; shortly afterwards, their baby dies of malnutrition. Nedda, who has sold the few meager things she had put together for a marriage which never took place, is left alone once more, destitute, blessing the dead that suffer no more.

It is, as can be imagined, a terse story, and one told with considerable restraint and economy of means: Nedda's bewilderment and anguish are depicted in a few, somber words; her love affair is barely hinted. The pivotal incidents of the story—first, the mother's death, then Nedda's own sense of loss, her willingness to take on any hard job so that she may support herself, her affair with Janu, her baby's death—are given no special prominence. They are registered almost casually, as though they were matters of simple fact. The story is not perfect; there is the artificial device of the story being told within a story, and there is a certain uneveness of tone. Verga shifts from the condescension of an urbane, humanitarian gentleman to the disinterestedness of a casual observer. This notwithstanding, we are moved by the sense of fatalism that pervades the whole tale, by Nedda's thoughtful conclusion that death is preferable to life. It is with Nedda that we enter the world of Verga's special primitives, capable of enormous sacrifices and unusual stoicism. His people appear from the outset as vanquished, defeated by the brute force of nature and by an egotism that respects no human values or principles. Their heroism is in their striving to find the strength to endure a life that offers little joy but imposes continual toil and suffering. Theirs is the heroism which in their most desperate and bleak moments permits them to find a stature and dignity possible to the characters of Greek tragedies.

Like "Nedda," the stories that Verga wrote during the following years, *Primavera* (*Primavera and Other Tales*), 1877, and *Vita dei campi* (*Life in the Fields*), 1880, are notable for their rare simplicity. Invariably, they revolve around the hardships or passions endured or experienced by Sicilians—laborers, farmhands, shepherds—all equally proud yet resigned to a wretched existence, wishing merely to live simply and quietly, enjoying whatever little satisfaction life can offer them. Their existence could hardly be more precarious: they live from day to day, constantly faced by a harsh nature, unforgiving and indifferent to the plight of humankind in a manner bound to recall the work of Giacomo Leopardi. The elements become more prominent in the stories; we become aware of how important the weather is since, as Thomas G. Bergin notes, "the *contadini* depend for their existence on the whim of the weather. . . . If the *annata* is good, all is well; if not, then those on the margin of society pay the price." Similarly, the role played by the animals becomes more important—the animals that are valuable assets, to be sure, but that also poignantly and silently reenact the unbelievably hopeless activity of Verga's peasants. They live like dogs, work like donkeys (which, in Italy, occupy the last place in the animal hierarchy); like horses, they exist purely to work the land, and like the sheep they take to pasture, day in and day out they must exhibit meekness of spirit and restrained behavior. At times, as Pina (in the story "The She-Wolf"), they are nicknamed after animals, and appropriately so in Pina's case, since the wolf is a treacherous, proud animal whose only allegiance is to itself. "The horses," Verga writes at one point, "are made to be sold;

similarly, the lambs are born to go to the slaughterhouse, and the clouds bring rain with them."

The world of Verga's primitives is distinguished by its simple feelings, its modest aspirations, where people, as Lia remarks in "Ieli" "act like animals . . . that scratch each other's neck," and where man, with no opportunity to educate himself, confesses, with Ieli, "I'm poor . . . I don't know anything."

A life of deprivations and poverty, of exploitation and betrayals can only produce, in the fiction of Verga at any rate, unhappiness and violence. The stories of *Life in the Fields* are replete with deaths, of violent deaths that represent the culmination of a heroic but unbearable despair. There is Alfio who kills his rival Turiddu in the famous "Cavalleria rusticana"; Ieli the shepherd who murders his boyhood pal, Don Alfonso, who has seduced Ieli's wife, Maria, and thus ruined his dream of a tranquil home; there is Nanni Lasca who slaughters the she-wolf with an ax and curses her afterward. Thus violence, murder, and fighting provide a dramatic contrast to the peace of mind Verga's heroes seek in vain. In a way, Rosso Malpelo, the protagonist of the story by the same title, presents the philosophy of the novelist's special world in no uncertain terms. Rosso, "a little brat whom nobody wanted around" in the stone quarry where his father lost his life for a handful of miserable tari, grows accustomed to the beatings his master and even his friends regularly administer upon his back. "In fact, he took the beatings without complaining, just like the donkeys that arch their backs, but go on doing things their own way." Rosso understands very well the reality of his condition. Speaking to his friend Frog, he says, "The donkey must be beaten, because he can't beat us; if he could, he'd smash us under his hoofs and rip our flesh apart." With Rosso Malpelo, we become aware that we are confronting a world of dog-eat-dog, ruled by a combination of power, personal interests, and crude egotism.

Thematically and stylistically, *Life in the Fields* is obviously an important work, whose significance is this time also theoretical. In the case of two short stories, "Fantasticheria" ("Reverie") and "L'amante di Gramigna" ("Gramigna's Mistress"), the novelist makes several revealing points about his poetics and, at the same time, announces the first novel of a cycle of five he had undertaken to write, a series he would eventually title "The Vanquished."

> When in the novel the affinity and the cohesion of its every part will be so complete that the process of creation remains a mystery like the development of human passions themselves, and the harmony of its forms will be so perfect, the sincerity of its reality so evident, its mode and reason for being so necessary that the hand of the artist will remain absolutely invisible, then it will have the stamp of a real happening and the work of art will seem to have produced itself, to have matured and to have grown spontaneously like a fact of nature, without maintaining any point of contact with its author, without the blemish of the sin of creation.

The statement has a familiar ring, for it echoes some of the programs and theories of French realists, particularly Flaubert. Much has been made of Verga's theory of impersonality, and justly so. In the history of the novel in Italy, his declaration is a true milestone. Today we are likely to be less impressed by theoretical pronouncements than by the discovery of a technique that succeeds in making a work of fiction truly original as well as believable and compelling. No matter how desperately the author may try to disappear from his fiction, he is always retraceable in the very people, landscapes, and actions his imagination has created. Perhaps Verga did not at all intend to formulate an ideal technique but rather to underscore the fact, which seems incontrovertible to us born and raised in a post-Henry James era, that, in order to sound authentic, real, *lived*, the novelist would have to do away with his customary clumsy treatments that made his characters puppets rather than independent creatures. We need not assume that this practice was limited to Italy, as it was, as has been pointed out by many critics in the past, a European trend. As Joseph Warren Beach put it in his admirable study of *Fiction in the Twentieth Century*, "The one thing that will impress you more than any other [in the modern novel] is the disappearance of the author. In Fielding and Scott, in Thackeray and George Eliot, the author is everywhere present in person to see that you are properly informed on all circumstances of the action, to explain the characters to you and to insure your forming the right opinion of them, to scatter nuggets of wisdom and good feeling along the course of the story, and to point out how, from the failures and successes of the characters, you may form a sane and right philosophy of conduct." Verga's position was one strikingly modern, for he believed that only by disappearing from his work would the novelist make his tale believable without question and give it a spontaneity and a truthfulness unattainable by conventional narrative techiques. Whether or not such worthy goals can really be attained by an objective, or impersonal kind of narrative, has become after Wayne C. Booth's brilliant book, *The Rhetoric of Fiction*, debatable to say the least. Nonetheless, it is difficult to deny that the obstrusive, moralizing role traditionally played by the author-narrator in the bulk of fiction up to that time was anything if not damaging to the illusion of reality each artist seeks to create in his work. Furthermore, the intrusions of the author were frequently but poor surrogates for an experience that, to ring true for the reader, needed to be dramatically presented. To quote Mr. Beach once more, "if the author succeeds in presenting his theme effectively . . . we shall not quarrel with his personal appearances. . . . Our main quarrel is with the author who makes his personal appearance a *substitute* for the artistic presentation of his subject, thinking that talking about it is equivalent to presenting it."

Verga's approach to fiction was to undergo some changes in the years that followed his Sicilian stories, and eventually blossomed in the Preface to *The House by the Medlar Tree* where he takes up his points from where the letter to Salvatore Farina (in "Reverie") had left off. The basic scheme of the cycle was contained in a single, illuminating sentence of the story just quoted. "Whenever one of those small, or weaker, or less cautious, or egotistical plebian actors decides to cut himself off from his own folk because of his yearning for the unknown, or his desire to better himself, or his curiosity to know the world, the world—voracious fish that it is—swallows him and all those nearest to him." This vision of man's fate was to be dramatically presented in *The House by the Medlar Tree* and in the four novels that were to be its sequel.

Verga himself gave a first account of his ambitious plan in a letter written to his friend Salvatore Paola, on April 21, 1878, defining his project a "fantasmagory of life's struggle, extending from the ragpicker to the minister of state and the artist, assuming all forms from ambition to avidity of profit, and lending itself to a thousand representations of the great, grotesque play of mankind, the providential struggle guiding humanity through all appetites, high and low, to its conquest of truth!" Each of the novels planned was to have its own special physiognomy, and each was to be self-contained. It took several years before Verga completed *The House by the Medlar Tree* and readied the manuscript for press. He saw it in print in 1881.

The reception accorded the novel was to be a grave disappointment to the Sicilian. Aside from a few favorable reviews—written for the most part by his friends—the publication of one of the finest novels of the century, and one of the most revolutionary works of fiction produced by the modern Italian imagination, was to pass practically unnoticed.

The conceptual framework of "The Vanquished" is tersely outlined in the Preface that accompanied *The House by the Medlar Tree*. Any reader wishing to gain some insights into Verga's quasi-Balzacian project must inevitably turn to such statements as the piece offers for his enlightenment.

"This story," Verga writes, "is the genuine and dispassionate study of how the first aspirations for well-being probably originate and develop in the humblest classes. It is the study of the perturbations brought into a family, that up to that point had lived a relative happy existence." The artist's intention was "to give a representation of reality as it actually was, or as it should have been," and to analyze "the mechanism of human passions." The range of his observation was to be all-inclusive, moving progressively from the lowest social class (a family of poor fishermen), to the bourgeoisie and ultimately to the aristocracy. The additional volumes that were to follow *I Malavoglia* were to bear the following titles: *Mastro-don Gesualdo*, *La Duchessa de Leyra* (*The Duchess of Leyra*), *L'onorevole Scipioni* (*The Honorable Scipioni*), and, finally *L'uomo di lusso* (*The Man of Wealth*). Each social class, with its unique aspirations and ambitions, its diverse life and ensuing world view, was to be depicted through the use of a narrative style wholly consonant with the social condition and the sophistication of its characters. A similarly tragic fate would constitute their common denominator, since the author envisioned the world as the same ground of battle, where today's winners would end up being tomorrow's losers. Notwithstanding the pseudo-scientific pretensions of such a plan, Verga succeeded admirably in creating two novels that are not in the least contrived.

Few stories could actually be simpler than the one told with consummate skill by Verga in *The House by the Medlar Tree*. It is a tale revolving around the many vicissitudes that strike a family of fishermen, the Malavoglia. In the course of the story, the heroes discover the meaning of death, defeat, moral degradation, fear, misery, and love. Somehow, thanks to the force that pulls them close to one another, they manage to survive the large and small crises regularly disrupting the rugged course of their existence, and rediscover and reassert the precious values inherited from their ancestors. Indeed, without such values, their universe would prove to be meaningless. Such a characterization of the essence of the novel is but a mere approxima-

tion to what it ultimately says. So rich and different are its
meanings that it lends itself to a variety of interpretations,
many of which are perfectly justified by the text. It can be
called the drama of a brave family, buffeted by misfortunes and doomed to much suffering before it can once
more experience the tranquillity for which it yearns; it can
be read as an absorbing representation of what life must
have been in many parts of the *Mezzogiorno* during the
last century (or in ours for that matter); it is also a tale of
the misery and trouble life brings to the human kind, and
how they are accepted, endured, and occasionally overcome by brave men. But the novel, because it is a great
work of art, manages to be all these things and many
more. Its manifold meanings can be uncovered not by the
insights of a single critic, or several critics, but by the
sensitivity of a reader capable of discerning and recognizing in the events of the book's plot a reflection and an
illumination of the destiny of man. Thus, the novel lends
itself to be read as a depiction of the perennial conflicts
between the new and the old generations; or of the restlessness every young person experiences when he faces life
on his own and grows disillusioned with a social, political,
and moral system and an order of values he can no longer
comprehend, because they fail to fill his needs and respond to his aspirations.

Grand and powerful, though by no means unusual, as
the themes of the book may be, it must be acknowledged
that what makes the novel an unusually fine work is its
style and technique; or, better stated, the manner in which
the form of the tale is one with its content. The problem
of style is one that has historically occupied every great
writer; hardly a poet or novelist has avoided a confrontation with this vital issue. It is clear (but, I hasten to add,
only to the reader capable of handling the novel in the
original), that Verga must have been faced by a number
of alternatives when he first thought of his cycle, and in
particular in the case of *The House by the Medlar Tree*.
The major choices no doubt were three: to use the literary
language he had inherited from his tradition (the lan-

guage of Manzoni's *The Betrothed*); or to deviate slightly from such a choice by injecting into the novel expressions, sayings, or isolated worlds drawn from the Sicilian dialect; or to write his book entirely in dialect. Of these alternatives, the last he considered the least desirable, as it would restrict his public to those possessing a mastery of the dialect. Moreover, neither of the other two possibilities satisfied him, although in some of his short stories he had indeed resorted to employing dialect words or local sayings whenever he felt that Italian was simply incapable of recapturing the nuances and force of the Sicilian expression.

Dissatisfied with the available linguistic options, he decided to embark on the road that was to lead him to the outright invention of a language capable of expressing the thoughts, feelings, and utterances of his Sicilian heroes in a manner that would be comprehensible to the reader untrained in the dialect. The course chosen was not without difficulties and special problems, for it demanded a thorough preparation of his part not unlike that necessary to Joyce in writing *Ulysses*. Verga was not only obliged to study anew the traditions, beliefs, and customs of the people he intended to fictionalize, but indeed the psychology of their language. In short, the speeches and thoughts of the characters had to be filtered by the author and translated, so to speak, into a language understandable to the general reader without losing the special flavor and cadence of their native dialect or of their personality. Ultimately, this operation was clearly one that required a reshaping of the literary language, cleansing it of its pomposity and artificiality, transforming it into the aptest expressive tool of characters who are ignorant peasants. Moreover, as Luigi Russo perceptively noted, he "gave a provincial coloring to the language of *The House by the Medlar Tree* through the images and proverbs of the town [of Aci Trezza], [and] through a choral syntax."

The problem of "how" the characters might speak or the novel be told was obviously intimately connected with a problem of structure. Up to that moment, the traditional novel in Italy was generally narrated by an omniscient author, (frequently occupying the role of the protagonist as well) who looked on the events from the outside, remaining a kind of special, partial observer. Another technique frequently used, especially in France, was that of the epistolary novel, of the type Verga himself had practiced in his early *Story of a Linnet*. With *The House by the Medlar Tree* Verga took a different path. He rejected both the role of the omniscient narrator and the possibility of identifying himself with one of the principal characters. The story he chose to tell is narrated from the *inside*, not by one but indirectly by *all* the personages of the novel. Every character is thus magically transformed into a narrator, each contributing something, with his unmistakable voice, to the description of the Malavoglia's woes. As Verga's most recent translator points out, "It is their voice that we hear telling the story; the entire novel is, so to speak, dialogued." Verga's technique is one based on direct and indirect discourse; we either hear the characters speak or we are told, by one of the characters, the essence of what has taken place. Indeed, what the characters say is often reported indirectly in a way that mirrors the spoken rather than written speech. The so-called minor characters often act as a chorus, whose function, much like a Greek tragedy, is to comment upon the dramatic events of the story.

Nowhere does Verga attempt to make a direct comment on, or judgment of, the action he describes, and much less does he try to influence the opinion of the reader. The method he selects is that of a novelist whose function must be deceptively limited to providing the information in as vivid and complete a manner as possible so the reader may see and judge for himself. In addition, in the novel seeing is combined with hearing. What we *hear* a character say, or what is said about him, enables us to recognize him by his personal idiosyncrasies, by his speech and action. Our insights into their quality as human beings are extended by frequent opinions and gossip offered by friends and relatives, whose conversations reveal an intimate, but never offensive, concern for life in the community. The unusual feat is accomplished by transporting us into the town of Aci Trezza, where we are forced to mingle with its inhabitants, learning about them from their own words. Their language is real and believable not because it flows effortlessly but because it remains highly consistent with their personality, their experience of life, their background—making use of a vocabulary that is drawn not from literature but from life itself, their occupation and interests.

The relatively few descriptive passages of *The House by the Medlar Tree*—such as the beautiful and lyrical opening of Chapter III or the melancholy paragraphs that close the book—are written as though they were in fact spoken by an unidentified villager whose manner of speech follows a pattern familiar to us since we have encountered it many times in the unfolding of the tale.

The novel's setting is kept purposely narrow: practically the entire story takes place in the town of Aci Trezza. Conversely, the cast of characters that meet at the house of the Malavoglia, at the town watershed, at the local inn, or just in the streets is comparatively large. Their heated, at times humorous, political conversations, their constant commentaries on the events of the day, their small business deals take place not in the intimacy of their homes but out in the open, on the landings, and in the streets. Everything in the novel helps create the illusion that we are in a small town: the small talk we hear, the provincial attitude of the peasants, the petty jealousies and nagging grievances, the unobstrusive manner in which some of the extraordinary or important happenings that take place in the mainland reach the town as faint echoes. Thus, for example, when word reaches them that Luca Malavoglia has died in the war, the news stuns the friends of the family, who express their disbelief and surprise by flatly affirming that the whole affair "is a lot of talk, just to sell newspapers." We are truly cut off not only from the continent but from history itself. We live a drama with many self-repeating acts, a drama whose heroes change their names but not their roles for they are all equally involved in the endless struggle for survival and further-ance of their own selfish interests. We are thrust into a world where misery is rampant and greed is frequently out of proportion with what is at stake; a world of hard work and sorrow accepted with resignation as the lot of man. In such a world there is little awareness of the tragic fact that, sooner or later, everyone will be overcome by the vicissitudes of life.

Religion, which permeates the whole of Manzoni's novel, is conspicuously absent here, except in the most perfunctory way. Left to their wits for centuries, the peo-ple of Aci Trezza have replaced a traditional faith in God with a stubborn confidence in their capacity to resolve the daily obstacles confronting them. The town's vicar, Gian-maria, is depicted as an observer equally unconcerned with the Malavoglia's troubles and the day-to-day hardships endured by the townsfolk. He performs his religious duties in a most perfunctory manner, with a minimum of faith in what he does and a maximum of speed. The ultimate reality, which for Manzoni had been a boundless faith in the Love and Justice of the Maker, is transformed, in the world of Verga, into a purely economic fact, a question of money and circumstances. This explains the frequent la-conic comments of its people, or young 'Ntoni's compul-sion to leave town in search of fortune after his family has repeatedly been struck by disaster.

The fate of the Malavoglia is a tragic one: one by one, it seems, they must bow their heads to an unpredictable destiny. Bastianazzo is the first to die in the first shipwreck of the family's boat, *La Provvidenza;* Luca loses his life while serving his country and fighting a war which few can believe is taking place; Lia becomes a woman of the streets and leaves town; *Comare* Maruzza dies of cholera during a frightening epidemic; and old 'Ntoni ends his life in a lonely hospital, after an existence marked by incredible toil.

Why is it that they must go down to their death or ruin so unjustly or so unnecessarily? The temptation is great to take the essence of the Preface literally, and explain their tragic end through their obstinate drive to improve their material lot. As it actually turns out, the family's speculation in a cargo of lupins proves to be the least serious offense to the Verghian code of life, and, as such, the element only remotely responsible for their subsequent woes. Their defeat is rooted not in their economic disasters, but in their betrayal of the religion of the home, as it has been called, in their having broken the tradition of steadfastness to an ancestral code. They have failed to abide by what the novelist elsewhere (in the story "Reverie") had defined as "the ideal of the oyster." Only the members of the family who truly believe in such an honorable ideal find the strength necessary to bear their heavy burden of grief. What gives Mastro 'Ntoni, Alessi, and Mena—the three people whose strength of character and allegiance to the code enables them to survive their ordeal—an unusual amount of vitality, fortitude, and resilience is their strong commitment to enduring human values: their unshakeable belief in the necessity of working hard, and above all honorably; their indestructible faith in the dignity of man; their joy of working as a unit; and their deep affection for the house by the medlar tree, which throughout the novel remains the center of family life, the most overt symbol of their attachment to life. When the house is lost to repay a debt, it becomes the ideal point of return for the Malavoglia.

The nature of Verga's impersonal technique excludes the presence of the customary portraits of characters we find so admirably done in Manzoni's novel. While the Milanese writer's method calls for a historical-moral approach to the problem of character presentation and analysis (can anyone forget the masterful, three-dimensional portraits of Don Abbondio, Fra Cristoforo, or the Nun of Monza?) Verga relies exclusively on a few bold strokes and details to give his heroes a quality and dimension we are not likely to forget. It is his economy of means coupled with the adroit device of allowing his characters to define themselves through their acts and utterances, complemented by the comments made by the other personages of the book, that constitutes one of the fresh and vital aspects of the work. Master 'Ntoni's first words in the story denote clearly what kind of an individual he is. He speaks frequently by way of proverbs and maxims, almost as a kind of oracle, and through his terse words, which in wisdom and an unflagging belief in the validity of human experience, we get a distinct feeling of what will prove to be the key issues of the story. "To pull an oar, the five fingers must work together"; or "Be satisfied with what your father made you, if nothing else you won't be a rascal." The other characters of the story are presented in very quick succession, in a manner that echoes a spoken rather than a literary style. There is old 'Ntoni's son, Bastianazzo, "who was big and burly" but "he'd put about directly when ordered and wouldn't blow his nose without his father's say-so"; then comes his wife Maruzza, called La Longa, a "tiny woman who kept busy weaving, salting anchovies and bearing children, like a good housewife." Then come their five children: 'Ntoni, "a big loafer of twenty"; Luca, "who . . . had more sense than his older brother"; Alessi, "a little snot nose, who was the spitting image of his grandfather"; and Lia, "who was not yet fish, flesh or fowl." Just a few words are sufficient to introduce, and in several profound ways anticipate, the character of the heroes, what they are capable of doing and how they will eventually turn out as human beings.

For generations the Malavoglia have lived in the same town, leading a modest but dignified existence, esteemed by the community as hard-working and industrious people. Theirs is a patriarchical family with the old grandfather, the respected leader, entrusted with the responsibility of making major decisions that will affect the course of their lives. It is he who holds the family together with his strength and wisdom, giving it a direction and a sense of purpose and stability, guiding its route as an experienced shipmaster. His wisdom, however, is not acquired through book learning but from life itself—from the understanding he has attained of the kind of duties and obligations he must exercise both with respect to himself and to his dear ones. Master 'Ntoni clings with rare tenacity to the moral relevance—the ethics, as it were—of the tenets guiding his life. In this sense, too, the proverbs and maxims through which he speaks serve to convey the meaning and intimate reasons for his actions. It is for the good of the family that he has contracted a debt with Uncle Crocefisso, known as Dumbbell, buying a cargo of lupins which he plans to take to the nearby town of Riposto. From there, a larger ship will transport it to the northern port of Trieste. But, during a storm, the family's boat is severely damaged, Bastianazzo and a helper Monico lose their lives, and the lupins are lost in the sea.

Soon, the credit extended by Uncle Crocefisso runs out. When the unpaid debt threatens to stain the family's good name, Master 'Ntoni first thinks of the possibility of resorting to legal maneuverings to invalidate the transaction (especially since the lupins were said to be spoiled), then sets himself to do whatever must be done to pay back the money he owes. But he suffers still more setbacks, and, after having exhausted all honest avenues open to him, he consents to give up his beloved house by the medlar tree and make good on his word.

Once the house is lost, Master 'Ntoni's goal becomes that of regaining possession of what has always been for the family the supreme symbol of unity and security. As Russo perceptively writes, "the house is not a harbor of peace and well-being; it is not a tranquil refuge of small egotism, but the small brown anthill to which the ants go back and onto which they cling, after the anguish of the comings and goings of their dispersion and storm." Gradually, the book becomes less a tale of a debt that honor demands be repaid, but a story of personal heroism, the account of the enormous sacrifices each member of the family willingly makes to retrieve a vital part of his way of life. The technique of Verga's narration is such that we remain only dimly aware of the passing of time—a thoroughly effective way to remind us that there is a larger dimension to the Malavoglia story, since their fate is but a continual cycle of disasters that only infrequently alternate with imperceptible gains. Suffering is, in the world of the Sicilian novelist, an ever-present condition no one can avoid. "The world," so comments at one point the impersonal voice of the narrator, "is packed with trouble: some get half, some get double, and the people who were outside in the yard kept looking at the sky for another bit of rain that would have been as welcome as bread."

Those who depart from the world of the living seem to be the most fortunate of the lot, for they will not have to confront the dread of moral or economic ruin. A bitter fate, charged with infinite toil and endless suffering, awaits those who live on. It is a fate that must be accepted, for the alternative is perhaps even gloomier. Thus, young 'Ntoni is thoroughly corrupted by the glamour and glitter of city life during his military tour of duty; back in his native town, he realizes that he has become estranged to its values and way of life. He rejects the possibility of working like the other members of the family, especially since he is convinced of the futility of the human struggle for survival by honest means. He takes up with the town's worst people, gets into trouble and is sentenced to jail for having stabbed the local customs official Don Michele (with whom he has a long standing grievance) who caught him smuggling coffee, sugar, and silk kerchiefs. As a result of seeing his oldest grandson brought to trial as a criminal, old 'Ntoni suffers a stroke and, at his insistence, is brought to the city hospital. There he dies a lonely death, shortly after Alessi has brought him the good news that the house by the medlar tree is once again about to be theirs. Alessi is the one who is destined to carry on the name and the tradition of the family; he is also the only one to experience the happiness of a good marriage. Mena, promised to Brasi Cipolla, sees her plans go up in smoke after the first setback of the boat. Later, she accepts to bear the brunt of the shame brought to the family by Lia's dishonorable behavior and turns down Alfio Mosca's request to marry him, despite the fact that she has always loved him. "I'm twenty-six and the time when I could get married has passed," she confesses sadly. She goes back to living in the old family house, where she takes up an attic room "waiting for Nunziata's children so she could mother them." The story will see young 'Ntoni back to his town after having completed his sentence. The single night he spends there, however, is sufficient to persuade him that it is impossible for any man to remain in a place full of bitter, haunting memories.

The novel's events are sparse and modest almost to the point of seeming trivial. It is one of the many achievements of the book, however, to show us that what it presents is no inconsequential struggle, but a dramatic battle that takes place, in a larger scale and on a vastly more complicated stage, in life as we know it. Only by viewing the book from a distance are we able to study its architecture and begin to discover the perfection of its design. There is both progress and continuity in the story. Whatever happens to its heroes manages to keep us in a continual state of suspense, even though we expect that our feelings will not be betrayed. In the world so starkly created by the imagination of Verga, man is resigned to his lot, even though he never gives up at least the hope of a material improvement of his condition. We are carefully led to the final climax through a series of ups and downs; by the time old 'Ntoni dies, we have been through events that have changed, in one way or another, every member of his family. The misfortunes that strike the Malavoglias are never sufficiently serious to destroy their dogged attachment to life, or their stubborn hope that there may still be something good in store for them. By the same token, their recoveries from their setbacks are never great enough to enable them to resolve their problems in any substantial way.

Tragic and comic touches alternate in the novel, for this is no bleak account of the numerous disasters that have hit the family and have destroyed its confidence in life itself, but a tale of the irony and humor of life. There is, to begin with, irony in the very name the Malavoglia bear, for far from their being full of ill-will as their nickname implies, they are conscientious and hard-working, and there is irony, too, in the name of their boat, which brings them not good luck or abundance but hardships and troubles. There is still another kind of irony in the fact that Don Michele, who is partly responsible for saving the life of Master 'Ntoni when he is brought back, seriously hurt, from the second shipwreck of the boat, is also the one who seduces Lia and is eventually responsible for sending young 'Ntoni to jail, thus contributing materially to the misery of the family. There is also a well-measured humor in Brasi Cipolla's falling prey to Mangicarubbe, a no-good woman with whom he takes up when his engagement with Mena is dissolved, and there is humor in Uncle Crocefisso's marriage with La Vespa, who delights in squandering the money he has painfully accumulated after years of speculations and usury.

Humor and irony successfully establish and enhance contrasts and vary the tone of the narrative; they do not decrease its fatalism, the inescapable absurdity of all its events. The question that faces us, and cannot be adequately answered, is: Why should the Malavoglias, upright, honest, hard-working and God-fearing, be so repeatedly and mercilessly struck by Fate? Is God, or nature, or another incomprehensible force responsible for their misery and misfortunes? Perhaps, as someone recently remarked, we transcend in the novel even a Leopardian type of pessimism, for we find ourselves in a universe where, discern as we do the difference between good and evil, no differentiation between them can actually be made. Who is better off: Master 'Ntoni, always striving but invariably defeated, or Rocco Spatu, the town's best specimen of the good-for-nothing who lives off the fat of the land, taking from it but never contributing anything in return? Prodded by his grandfather to work hard and to be thankful for what he has, young 'Ntoni puts his problem into perspective by answering

> "But are you people living any better than I am, with all your working and useless struggling? It's our cursed lot, that's what it is! You see how worn out you are, you look

like a fiddle bow, and you've grown old always liking the same life! And now, what have you got? You people don't know the world, you're like kittens with their eyes still closed. Do you eat the fish you catch? Do you know for whom you work, from Monday to Saturday, and for whom you've worn yourself out so that they wouldn't even take you in at the hospital? For the people who never do a lick of work, and have piles of money. That's who you're working for. . . . Ah, by the book of the thieving Judas, what a miserable fate!"

'Ntoni's rebellion, which climaxes in his eventual downfall, and Lia's placid surrender to her sexual instincts represent an answer of sorts, however inconclusive and ultimately damaging to their well-being, to the wretchedness humans are asked to accept without protest as an inescapable part of their condition. Unconsciously, both 'Ntoni and Lia aspire to joining the ranks of those who, like Piedipapera and Uncle Crocefisso, have succeeded in scoring a victory in the harsh struggle of existence. What they have neglected to comprehend is that in life no victory is ever total or permanent, and in Verga's scheme of life today's winners will turn out to be tomorrow's vanquished. In the novel, only the losers elicit our sympathy, less because they are the underdogs than because they go down to defeat—or barely manage to survive their ordeal—without surrendering their obstinate faith in those moral values that have always given a measure of coherence and meaning to what would otherwise be a senseless affair.

Unlike Manzoni, Verga offers no answers to the eternal riddle of existence, no program of action, no staunch commitment to a religious faith. In some ways, Verga has something in common with Albert Camus in indirectly asserting that only a genuine solidarity with other human beings is ultimately capable of alleviating, and rendering more bearable, the suffering and tragedy that mankind has to endure.

Mastro-don Gesualdo, the second and last novel completed by Verga as part of his projected cycle, is infinitely more complex than *The House by the Medlar Tree* but less successful and satisfying, despite its many fine pages and excellent episodes. It is, from the point of view of scheme, the attempt to carry on to a higher social class the same basic struggle we find in the tale of the Malavoglias—a struggle we know must end in defeat, for an inimical fate sternly denies man any possibility of trespassing the boundaries of his inherited condition. The hero of the novel is a contractor, Mastro-don Gesualdo Motta, who, by the sweat of his brow, has been able to free himself from the shackles of his humble origin, achieving an enviably comfortable economic status. The sacrifices he has made are as numerous as the calculating deals that have enabled him to become a wealthy man. Yet, the material success he has achieved at such a hard price does not prevent his ultimate failure, for the scheme must be fulfilled; the victories of today beget the defeats of tomorrow.

From a proletarian, humble, primitive milieu, Verga moves in the second novel to a bourgeois society, the world of businessmen, and *nouveaux riches*. Such a world obviously requires a new language in order that its yearnings, aspirations, and quality might be expressed and studied in a manner consonant with its character. But the style Verga employs in the book is disappointing for it lacks the freshness, inventiveness, and vitality of his earlier novel.

Much like *The House by the Medlar Tree*, the great theme of *Mastro-don Gesualdo*—the struggle for property and the consequences of wealth—is adumbrated in a short piece titled "La roba." The narrative, barely six pages long, can hardly be classified as a short story, since it does not revolve around an unusual event, but merely gives us a brief glimpse of its protagonist, Don Mazzarò, and his incredible appetite for possessions through which he believes he can achieve not only a secure position but happiness as well. *Mastro-don Gesualdo* repeats, in a larger and more involved social context, much the same struggle of Don Mazzarò. He incarnates the same human greed and drive for material possessions, his acceptance of a system of values that, devoid as they are of any real need of human solidarity, ultimately contribute to his psychological, financial, and physical ruin. In some ways Mastro-don Gesualdo might be seen as an extension of sorts of Lia and 'Ntoni Malavoglia, and their yearnings to improve their lot even at the cost of becoming corrupt or leaving the beloved house by the medlar tree. Unlike them, Gesualdo has indeed managed to amass a veritable fortune; yet his fate is not different from theirs. Gesualdo is a temporary winner in the human struggle to conquer his environment and overcome the restrictions of his social class, and yet he ends a defeated man. His life of toil and loneliness, amidst people he mistrusts and does not love, ends in a humiliating failure after he realizes that the wealth so painfully accumulated brings him no comfort whatever. Indeed, his money far from giving him the tranquillity, respect, and contentment he had hoped for, causes him misery and discontent compounded by the scorn heaped upon him when his health takes a severe turn for the worse and he approaches death. He ends his days in a house he abhors, without proper medical attention, cheated by his own family, who patiently waits for his death to squander the property he has accumulated—a true alienated man.

Unlike *The House by the Medlar Tree*, where the entire community of Aci Trezza is skillfully used by the novelist to tell his tale, and plays a vital role in the illusion that the drama is actually being lived and recounted by several people, in *Mastro-don Gesualdo* we have a hero and a cast of characters that are clearly defined and fully developed. Through four successive stages encompassing a period of approximately two and one-half decades (the story is set btween 1820 and 1846), we are shown the rise and fall of a man in search of a false god: money. "Property," Luigi Russo writes, "is no longer idolized for its own sake, but as a complex symbol of life, as a sentiment of labor, as a complacency of a constructive astuteness, as a sensuality of possession, an indiscriminate desire of survival and immortality." "You are good and beautiful!"

shouts Don Gesualdo to his wife during his wedding night, "Fine stuff . . . fine stuff you are!" The English translation cannot help its failing us at this point, however, for it hardly conveys the materialistic, almost vulgar connotations of the word *roba*, whose meaning is often property, goods, possessions ostentatiously displayed or enviously desired. Verga's choice is very apt here and elsewhere, and, after repeated usage, it becomes a leitmotiv of the novel that might well be called a hymn to real estate, to man's greed for things, yet another meaning of *la roba*. So intense is the impelling necessity to accumulate property—more specifically, land and grains—and so thoroughly does it pervade every one of the episodes in the story that the values of society can no longer be comprehended except in the coarsest material terms. If, as Harry Levin has reminded us in his study *The Gates of Horn*, realism etymologically means "thing-ism," then *Mastro-don Gesualdo* must be considered the realistic Italian novel par excellence. It is understandable that business transactions should be made for the sake of monetary gains, since this is an ancient practice and cornerstone of commerce since time immemorial. But in Verga's novel, every human action, from the most personal and delicate arrangement for matrimony to the most trivial family relationship is solely determined by money. "Whoever has money is right," proclaims the canon priest Lupi; and Baron Zacco, in another context, dryly observes: "Everyone is out for his own interest. . . . Nowadays interests come before family relations."

Mastro-don Gesualdo's failure cannot be attributed to his miscalculations or bad judgment in his business any more than the plight of the Malavoglia family may be explained by its drive to improve its lot. In both novels, Verga is in essence repeating the same theme, restating his view in different words, a view so simply synthesized in the expression "You can't graft peaches on an olive tree." If Mastro-don Gesualdo has done anything wrong, his major sin is that he has betrayed, by his actions and by his strivings, the goodness, simplicity, and worth of that background he has fiercely fought to eradicate from his personal history. His entire existence has been planned to insert himself into a social class to which he aspires but that would hardly tolerate him under other circumstances. Thus, he marries Bianca Trao, even though she has been seduced by her young cousin, Baron Nini Rubiera, because he realizes that it is necessary to marry a "name" in order to achieve a certain prestige in business circles; he sends his daughter Isabella to the Santa Maria [Boarding] School even before she is five years old, hoping that by so doing she will receive an education that will enable them to cancel his humble origin—only to discover that her school companions, well aware of her situation, ridicule her, tease her, and jeer her. It is understandable that, in view of such a situation, all human rapports should be conducted with the ultimate scope of exploiting and using people as means, not as ends in themselves. Indeed, Verga's characters live in a world where *la roba* is the only meaningful, lasting symbol of reality, the only available expression of power, prestige, and importance, the sole instrument capable of shaping the character and destiny of the individual, the only means through which the very course of history can be changed. In the novel, property becomes the focal point of reference, the element that propels people into prominence, hence giving them dignity and purpose. In Mastro-don Gesualdo's case, and in the Baroness Ribiera's, *la roba* attains the kind of meaning the old house had for the Malavoglia family. "Listen," warns Baron Zacco shortly before the wedding of Gesualdo and Bianca is to take place, "today the world belongs to those who have money."

Not everyone is possessed by the greed for riches, even when the purpose of wealth is not necessarily to acquire more power but to be used as an instrument to receive affection. Gesualdo's faithful servant, Diodata, for example, is hopelessly in love with her master; yet hers is a love that Verga aptly compares to that of an obedient, faithful dog. She has witnessed the slow, difficult rise of Don Gesualdo; she has been with him in spirit and in person every inch of his climb up the social ladder, up to the peak of what he can aspire—affluence and meaning—and finds herself brushed aside through his insensitivity and calculations. Although hurt and slighted, she returns to him in his dying days to assist him in his illnesses (among them, cholera contracted after his wife's death) in the tormenting and painful last hours of his life. Mastro Nunzio, Don Gesualdo's father, is another character who silently and regretfully is forced to watch over the inevitable march toward the final total rejection of those values he had treasured so highly. He scorns his son's futile attempts to be what he clearly is not, and can never be, and reminds him of his humble origin: "Your mother's name was Rosaria," he says, looking at his grandchild Isabella. Likewise, he is ready to frustrate the attempts his friends and relatives make to turn him into something he cannot be. "I was not born to live among rich people," Mastro Nunzio reminds his son. "My name is Mastro Nunzio," he proudly but modestly tells Baron Zucco, and "I don't put on my son's airs."

With all his hunger for material possession, Don Gesualdo is neither incapable of yearning for affection and love, nor does he forget the meaning and implications of his condition. As Verga presents him to us, he is able to understand the agony and toil his riches have cost him, and is equally sensitive both to the power made possible by money and to the "poetry of working" to accumulate the wealth he so obstinately wants. Precisely because of the way in which the author presents his hero to us, when the decay and disintegration of his empire begins one feels more sympathetic toward his defeat. Don Gesualdo, victim of a cancer-like disease that wastes him away, ever so slowly, is turned into a poignant creature, himself an impotent witness to the despicable manner in which his son-in-law devours his substance. Ultimately even money, yes the money he had so preciously treasured, becomes meaningless and absurd when its limitations are forcibly understood: "Money! You can none of you take your eyes off the money I've earned! What good is it to me if I can't buy even my health? A lot of bitterness it's brought me—always!" Indeed, as Gaetano Mariani lucidly put it, "*la roba* has induced him to betray his origins, *la roba* will alienate his father's love, and all his relatives who will end by dragging him to court, *la roba* will draw Don Gesualdo away from his daughter, who through foolish ambition he has educated like a noble girl, tying her to a noble husband who marries her for her dowry: all his life, built on *la roba*, is destroyed by *la roba*."

Because his true allegiance is to property, Don Gesualdo must endure the loneliness of a man who lives only to work, and works only to accumulate money, despised by the aristocrats, scorned by his rich relatives, hated by his competitors, and envied by the people: "Everyone was against him because he was rich. . . . Everyone conjured against him. . . . Now everyone deserted him." As the prototype of the materialistic man, Don Gesualdo must learn the meaning of the importance of people only when he loses them: his wife dies in the cholera epidemic, his father dies of old age, his daughter marries a nobleman who has nothing but contempt for his father-in-law and everything he is and stands for. After his wife passes away, Don Gesualdo's fortune declines rapidly, and, while he is not one to surrender easily, still the going is tough. His illness administers the *coup de grâce*: confined to his bed and incapable of personally supervising his affairs, he slowly understands that there is no longer any hope for him. He dies knowing that no one has really understood him, or indeed has understood what his property, his beloved *roba* for which he had sacrificed the best years of his life, really means to him.

7   MATILDE SERAO:
THE CHRONICLER OF MEMORY

IN THE SECOND HALF of the nineteenth century the novel in
Italy becomes an instrument that permits the writer to be
directly involved in the immensely vital task of discovering
his own country and to pinpoint the true essence of its
manifold reality. At this particular juncture, the majority
of writers do not pay the customary tributes to yesterday's
glorious exploits, but indeed begin to feel the wretchedness of today's conditions. The eye is not trained on the
past, but on the present; not on what *should* be, but on
what *is*. Such a stance produces not confessions or diaries,
but what amounts to powerful indictments of the evils,
injustices, and inequities of a social structure whose flaws
are exposed for everyone to see. One is almost tempted to
call much of the fiction produced in the latter 1800's a
literature of protest, deeply imbued with humanitarian
views and its aim, the preparation of ground for sorely
needed social reforms. The French influence is here at
once obvious: the works of de Maupassant, the Goncourt
brothers, Bourget, and Zola are widely read and passion-
ately discussed. An imposing number of writers seem to be
taken by a frenzy to resort to scientific methods to document their treatments of reality. Today we look with
suspicion on any attempt to dissect the complexity of life
as though it were a cadaver, or submit it to a laboratory
analysis and separate its ingredients to get a firm diagnosis
of its ills. Yet, we can hardly refrain from appreciating the
concerted effort of nineteenth-century novelists to grope

toward a more valid statement about the true causes of human misery, vices, and unhappiness by examining the social, economic, and psychological factors that affect human existence. In Italy, as in France, Taine's theory of *la race, le milieu* et *le moment* reigns supreme; and for several years the effort of many an artist is bent on trying to seize some of the unexplicable mysteries of life as though it were a plant or a body the author-turned-scientist could somehow dissect.

Fundamentally, such a prevalent situation had little visible effect on Serao, for whom literary theories or manifestoes held slight interest. As one of her critics has written, "Realism or naturalism . . . lose at once their worth on the concrete page. They are closer to an acceptance of a successful fashion than to a solid faith, closer to a provincial [sort of] realism than to a scientific or philosophical myth."

One of the most significant chapters in the history of the Italian novel of this period is written not in the avant-garde cities of Florence and Milan, which has traditionally served as rallying points for artists and intellectuals, but in Naples. It is in that socially and politically backward city that Italy's talented minds spring like flowers and produce the important works of criticism, philosophy, poetry, and fiction of the latter 1800's. The explanations offered for this unusual situation are numerous—too many in fact to be reported let alone discussed here—but perhaps Camillo Boito's, the Milanese disheveled poet, is the most persuasive for it centers on the very temperament of the Neapolitan. If art is "labor," he stated, "this is not true in Naples. The Neapolitan has the temperament of the artist. Ready to capture the beauty or the ridiculousness of things; perspicacious and mobile; impetuous in expressing his own feelings, but capable of quickly dominating or hiding them for a long time; very subtle in weaving explanations for everyone ['s actions] and for his own. He is a mixture of cold philosophy and burning sensuality. He has, in sum, all the qualities of the artist, both good and bad, in fact all good because they serve art."

Among the many writers who made of the South their particular cosmos several commend themselves to today's reader. The most representative and interesting of these are Matilde Serao, Federico De Roberto and Grazia Deledda.

Matilde Serao, born in Patras, Greece, in 1856, of a Greek mother and Neapolitan father, was at once the most prolific and perhaps the least significant of the three. Yet, so fully did she identify herself with her adopted city that she eventually became a sensitive observer and painter of the hope and despair of Naples. Indeed, the striking quality of Serao, telegraph operator and teacher who turned to fiction and journalism with a passionate zeal for changing a dreadful reality, is her uncanny ability to capture realistically the spirit of a tormented city. Her own feelings about the meaning of being raised in a squalid city moved her to record for herself and posterity the absurdity of an existence that always held for her a spark of poetry. "I dig into my memory," she wrote once, "in my memory where my remembrances are placed in successive strata, as layers of geological life on the terrestrial crust, and I give you my notes just as I find them, without reconstructing imaginary animals. . . . From the very first day I began to write, I have never wished or known to be anything else if not a faithful and humble chronicler of my memory. I entrusted myself to my instincts, and I do not believe I have ever been betrayed by them."

Just what may legitimately be said to constitute Serao's valid work was a question partially resolved in 1944, when Pietro Pancrazi produced a two-volume anthology of her finest pages culled from a production totaling over forty volumes. While the majority of Serao's readers acknowledge that some of her books have retained their originality and impact despite the passing of time, only a few critics have shown a willingness to take a fresh look at a writer so distinctly representative of the second half of the nineteenth century and to determine the extent of her role in the development of new narrative techniques.

It has frequently been said in the past that she loved

Naples, and that she sought to depict her favorite city for herself and posterity. However true this might be, what matters is not that she described life in Naples in a manner that is at once candid and poetic, but that she succeeded in seeing—and seizing—the opportunity of making Naples a subject of poetry. To put it in Gino Doria's words, "she understood Naples as material for art, in a new manner, imitated after her but never equalled let alone surpassed. She was Neapolitan, although born elsewhere, truly Neapolitan by instinct, feeling, habit." Whenever she wrote about the kind of life she knew intimately, she invariably reached striking results. Her fiction abounds with characters that are colorful, believable, and deeply human. Her main springs of inspiration were the poverty she saw everyday—which she feared to be beyond the average man's ability to conquer—and feminine passions, which she knew with equal certainty to be always strong and difficult to control.

Throughout a life that was particularly productive and that never lacked a moment of excitement, Serao sought to describe with the feeling of a reformer, the spirit of a humanitarian, and the accuracy of detail of the great realistic painters to whom she has often been compared, the simple, tragic life of Naples. She portrayed dozens of characters from the petite bourgeoisie and the working class—small shopkeepers, white collar employees, artisans, teachers, street vendors, house servants—struggling to exist in the midst of poverty. During the first fifteen years of her long literary career, from 1878 to her death in 1927, she wrote her best books and proved to be an indefatigable observer of the life and feelings, the passions and fears of human beings who, despite their humble origins, appear nobler and braver thanks to the heroism they display in the simple act of living.

The heroes of her fiction are plain, lowly, destitute, and almost invariably exploited human beings, living an existence bordering on the hopeless and redeemed only by their awareness of their circumstances and their attempts to overcome them. She set her characters in their natural habitat—the hovels, the crowded, dim, filthy *bassi* that can still be seen and serve as constant reminders that not all is well in today's affluent Italy. Her world is limited, to be sure; but it is so only because her sensitivity could respond—or respond best—to certain facets of a human being's life: misery, illusions, hopelessness, tenderness toward one's neighbor. She perceived that among the suffering creatures of her universe those who most desperately needed compassionate understanding were the youths and the children. Serao's best pages are, indeed, about children, their little worlds of dreams, hopes, and expectations. Her distinguishing traits are a profound empathy for the wretchedness of the existence most people must endure, and an almost voracious appetite for details that served her to record, faithfully and as completely as possible, the incredible happenings that give life its tragic overtones.

Serao did not conceive of fiction as an art form, and much less as something that could amuse people, but as a mission; writing for her could not, therefore, be simply an aesthetic activity. Indeed, writing remained always a downright curse, and to the end of her days she was haunted by the demon of her imagination and by the urge to put on paper what she saw and felt about the world. So strong was this compulsion that it frequently denied her the vital detachment of an artist wishing to create an independent world. The sense of urgency under which she composed her books robbed her of the time and patience needed to allow one's writing to remain in a desk drawer long enough to be ready for the eventual tiring and rigorous revisions. Had she chosen to take this difficult road what her books would no doubt have lost in spontaneity and freshness, they would have gained in stylistic and structural precision.

The bulk of her early production was to a large extent inspired by her direct experiences. Thus, after a stint working as a telegraph operator and as a teacher, she composed "Telegrafi di Stato" ("State Telegraphs"), and *Scuola Normale Femminile* (*Women's Normal School*),

and the other stories collected in *Il romanzo della fan-
ciulla* (*The Romance of a Young Girl*). Both books are
notable not merely for the impressive accuracy with which
they depict a side of life generally ignored by Serao's
contemporary writers but for a structure that was to become typical of the author's later books. Both are devoid
of a formal plot and are in essence a series of *bozzetti*, or
sketches, short episodes through which Serao gives a sense
of unity to her little world. Her aim is less to set individual
characters in unusual situations than to study the particular milieu in which their ills became increasingly more
serious. Gradually, Serao devoted more and more attention not just to these aspects to life in Naples that caught
her eye, but to the vices and flaws in the temperament of
its inhabitants that were ultimately responsible for their
misfortunes and ruin. Seldom has any writer in modern
Italy recreated so successfully the strange and seemingly
uncontrollable vice of gambling that is in the very blood
of poor people: "Terno secco" and *Il paese di Cuccagna*
(*The Land of Cockayne*) are absorbing treatments of the
theme of gambling. The former is a short story that revolves around a mother and daughter and their maid,
living very modestly without ever neglecting to show kind-
ness and generosity toward their neighbors. One day the
maid finds three numbers written on a small piece of
paper; they are the numbers her mistress intended to play
that week on the national lottery, but is unable to do so
because she no longer has sufficient money for that purpose. As it turns out, the maid gives the numbers to her
numerous friends and acquaintances, and the three numbers are among those that are drawn that week. Everyone
wins substantial amounts of money, except the *signora*,
who had preferred spending her last lire to purchase some
drawing material for her daughter.

Il paese di Cuccagna has frequently been called Serao's
best work and the book to which she owes her reputation.
It is at once a badly constructed novel and a rather intriguing sample of the kind of fiction Serao could write with
ease. It is a narrative without a strongly stated, or a

happily resolved plot, for indeed it ends by being a series of connected but episodic *bozzetti*. The most impressive side of the novel is not in the characterization, or in the colorfulness of its episodes, but in the manner it shows what happens not just to a particular social class but to an entire society, corrupted by an incurably ill with a malaise called gambling. The cancerous disease degrades and slowly destroys practically all the values and goals of life. The principal character of the novel is a Marquis Cavalcanti who, in his dedication to restoring the family's squandered estate, makes life all but unbearable for his daughter Bianca Maria, from whom he hopes to extract the winning combination at the national lottery that will permit him to recover his lost fortune. The tableau gets its rich colors, reminding one of Goya's paintings, not from the private happenings of the Cavalcanti family or Bianca Maria's tragic end, but from the picturesque pageants that periodically take place in Naples—the Festival of the Roses; the celebration and processions in honor of the town's patron, Saint Gennaro; the extraction of the lottery numbers every Saturday and the subsequent announcement of the few fortunate winners, for whom life will henceforth be less tragic, less desolate, and more secure, at least while the money holds out.

Realism, "realism of [man's] body and spirit," as she dubbed it, and irony were Serao's most effective narrative modes. When she uses them with a total awareness of their possibilities, she reaches unusual effects. Too often, unfortunately, she succumbs to the inordinate descriptions of things, people, facts, festivities, small talk—all the elements of Neapolitan life—that transform her narrative into a catalog *sui generis*, where the important element of selection is noticeably absent. Only rarely in her numerous books does she exercise a commendable control over her material, and the results are then short of extraordinary.

Exemplary, in this respect, is the novella *Storia di due anime* (*Story of Two Souls*), one of the finest and most moving stories Serao produced in her best period. The hero of the tale is Domenico Maresca, affectionately nicknamed Mimi, a hard-working, honest, talented statuette maker. Artistic and enchanting religious reproductions, the finest in Italy, come from his cluttered, dim, dusty little shop to take their place in churches everywhere. Gelsomina, a poor girl who is a faithful admirer of Mimi's craftsmanship, is deeply in love with him and fervently aspires to become his lifelong companion. But Domenico's eyes are turned toward Anna Dentale, the beautiful daughter of a formerly wealthy man; eventually Anna accedes to Domenico's request and becomes his wife. Their marriage, however, proves to be far from happy. Domenico is scorned by his father-in-law and rejected by his wife, who appreciates neither his devotion, nor his inept lovemaking. One day, Mimi finds himself alone. His wife has run off, taking his savings, his few valuables, and the vestments and jewels bedecking the life-sized statue of a Madonna commissioned by a wealthy stranger and ready to be delivered; Domenico is now a ruined man. The final irony of the story is provided by the return of Gelsomina, who, unable to support herself and to console herself for the loss of Domenico, has become a prostitute. The two reminisce about the innocent love of their youth, and only then do they realize how senseless their existence has been. Both have failed as human beings, and their tale is typical in that it has encompassed the betrayals and disappointments that strike those who fail to appreciate the opportunity to be happy, or those who demand of life more than they deserve or have the right to expect.

In the majority of her works, Serao used Naples, a poverty-stricken but generous city, as the setting for her tales. Only after a real voyage to Rome, where she and her husband, the renowned journalist and critic Edoardo Scarfoglio, resided for many years, did she compose books with a different setting and themes. *La conquista di Roma* (*The Conquest of Rome*) and *Vita e avventure di Riccardo Jonna* (*Life and Adventures of Richard Jonna*) were inspired by Serao's new experience in political and journalistic circles. Yet, whether her stories are strictly fictitious or, as in the case of *Il ventre di Napoli* (*The Bowels of*

Naples), moving and powerful reportage disguised as fiction, the focus of her interest remains the woman. Only in recent times have the qualities and weaknesses of feminine temperament been analyzed with a perception and knowledge typical of Serao. Women in love, women betrayed—in their dreams or reality—women fighting against other women for a man, women living in the lonely awareness that they will never marry; these are the true heroines of Serao's fictitious world. She has left behind a rich, if uneven, legacy of knowledge of the second sex and of the reality that was Naples in modern times—a legacy of which Italian letters can still be proud. "In a century's time," has written the critic Pietro Pancrazi, "if we should no longer know anything about Naples, [her] books should be sufficient to resuscitate it."

8   BETWEEN MYSTICISM
AND SCIENCE:
ANTONIO FOGAZZARO

AMONG THE MANY embarassing statements that can still be read in most manuals of Italian literary history, there is one boldly proclaiming the fact that Antonio Fogazzaro is not only a master storyteller, a gifted and prolific novelist, but also the author of a work of fiction that ranks second only to Manzoni's *The Betrothed*. That such an exaggerated estimate should have been made at all is attributable both to the incapacity of the general reader to challenge prevailing critical views and to the tendency of a school of criticism to foster old prejudices and worn myths rather than to restudy the works of the past in the light of a changed sensibility. By virtue of what passed for an act of mature, responsible critical judgment, Fogazzaro has, in the main, managed to retain a prominent position in the literary firmament of his country. Lately, however, a spirited, alert, and inquisitive nucleus of critics whose approach to literature ranges all the way from the Marxist to stylistic analysis has begun a new appraisal of the writer from Vicenza, with the result that, as the philologist Robert Hall, Jr. regretfully observes, "[Fogazzaro's] work has undergone an extraordinary devaluation."

On the surface, it is undeniable that those staunch admirers of Fogazzaro who claim that his best novel, *Piccolo mondo antico* (London, 1962; *The Little World of the Past*) is written in the great Manzonian tradition have a valid point. After all, they point out, the same undercurrents of religiosity and patriotism discernible in

The Betrothed are also tangibly present in Fogazzaro's novels. There is nothing wrong, to be sure, with his political views which, in fact, are both honorable and liberal for their time, or with his religious stance, however much it may lack the serenity and deep conviction of the Milanese writer. The problem, as we shall see, was that Fogazzaro's uncertainties generated a dogmatic representation of a religious vision and led him to facile categorizations of his country's political history. As a result, his novels tend to be overdramatic and unconvincing both as fiction and as treatments of central issues.

From the stylistic point of view, Fogazzaro is once more something of a disappointing writer. Obviously concerned with the problem of making his fictional characters believable, he sought to vary the tone of his narrative and their speeches by using, from time to time, words and expressions proper to the locale, a meager and unsatisfactory concession to the impelling necessity of bringing fiction closer to reality. By and large, Fogazzaro's characters speak in a lofty, literary, cultivated tone to the point that they give the impression of being not people but self-conscious artists, careful to measure every word and gesture so as to be faithful to the ideal image of themselves they wish to create. In this sense, indeed, it is fitting to speak of the Fogazzarian hero as foreshadowing the morbid, sensual, refined character that occupies the central position in the decadent novel of the turn of the century. Such strictures, however, must not, and are not intended to, deny the author's gift for creating dialogue. As Antonio Piromalli has justly observed, the crisp, warm, racy language used by Fogazzaro's personages make him closer to Goldoni than to Manzoni, as the playwright had an uncanny skill for capturing the music and diversities of dialogue.

When confronted by Fogazzaro's major novels, particularly those that by virtue of their themes and settings stake a claim on historical accuracy, today's reader is justifiably puzzled. Were the people of the nineteenth century so naïve and so conformist as to seem nothing more than stereotypes as Fogazzaro painted them? Were they as sharply, but as inconclusively, divided in their politics as *The Little World of the Past* makes us believe? Is Fogazzaro's depiction of the Church's position vis-à-vis the question of national unification true to life and hence historically accurate? When examined purely as a work of the imagination, Fogazzaro's masterpiece presents further problems: was his failure to create characters believable as real human beings and as the intellectuals they are supposed to be, attributable to a lack of perspective over his material, a mistaken concept of the nature of fiction, or a downright artistic ineptness? Serious questions such as these simply must be answered if we are to understand what Fogazzaro represents in the development of the novel in modern Italy, and what constitutes the lasting meaning of the books he wrote.

On the strength of the wide success and popularity his novels have enjoyed through the better part of our own century, Fogazzaro seems to occupy a prominent spot on the literary map of his country. When the quality and vision of his writing are more closely studied, however, he is bound to appear substantially less important to the point that he must be considered a writer doomed to have, among fellow novelists, some admirers but few imitators, and yet deserving a niche of his own.

When set against his contemporaries, principally Verga, Svevo, and Pirandello, the personality, interests, and orientation of Fogazzaro come into sharp relief. Although, like Verga, Fogazzaro was born into the upper bourgeoisie, unlike him he never showed much interest in, or sympathy for, the plight of the peasantry. Indeed, there is some evidence pointing to his contempt for the masses, less because of their primitive ruggedness than for their inherent weaknesses that made them easy preys of political manipulation. Unlike Verga, Fogazzaro did not set out to rejuvenate the literary language, but remained content to accept the Manzonian prose style he had inherited from the tradition—a model he enriched horizontally rather vertically by extending its expressiveness into other unexplored areas of human experience.

The similarities between the two northern writers, when they exist, are superficial. Unlike Manzoni, who was also obsessed by the great question of faith in God, Fogazzaro affords little freedom to his characters, so that they may become autonomous creatures, moving amidst errors, blunders, and short-lived victories, toward their goal in life which is self-fulfillment and happiness. When his many trials are finally over Renzo in *The Betrothed* has indeed learned a great deal from his varied experiences—even if the contemporary reader is apt to find the hero's conclusions far from elevating. Franco Maironi (the protagonist of *The Little World of the Past*), on the other hand, seems to be interested only in ascertaining whether his views were right and, fully persuaded of the correctness of his position in matters of faith, is able to reach his destination unscarred and, I believe, also largely unchanged as a man. Both Manzoni and Fogazzaro have a natural disposition for humor. But where in Manzoni humor is the creation of a mind capable of unusual observation of human behavior and of an extreme tolerance toward man's weaknesses, in Fogazzaro it generates from, and is generally resolved through, a facile ability to mimic the modes of speech and behavior of the people from his own native region—a factor that tends to limit his appeal and confers to his particular brand of humor a provincial tone.

Time and again, Fogazzaro focused on what he properly recognized to be the prime socio-political and religious issues of his time and intellectualized them. Unlike Svevo, however, he lacked the intuitiveness to probe into their minds and depict what made them love, believe, or suffer. He lost sight of the human dimension of his characters, and turned them into examples that made his case for all the noble things in life—family, fatherland, and God— more desirable and valid. Unlike Pirandello, and although he himself was torn by doubts and conflicts between opposite desires, he described but never closely studied the texture of his characters' lives, never haunted them with the possibility of unorthodox and dangerous alternatives. Rather, he chose to resolve their dilemmas (which were but a projection of his own) through a tranquil, but unpersuasive submission to the dogma of his Church.

Born in Vicenza in 1842, trained by Abbé Giacomo Zanella, himself a sensitive and learned poet, Fogazzaro took his law degree in 1864, practiced law for barely two years and, shortly after his marriage in 1866, turned to writing as a full-time activity. Although his first books were well received, he had to wait until 1885 and the publication of his *Daniele Cortis*—his second novel and fourth book—to receive the first critical accolades. For the next twenty-five years he remained the literary idol of the middle class, a fact that seems hardly extraordinary today. By reason of his birth, education, and interests, Fogazzaro was in fact eminently bourgeois, and as such he concentrated on portraying a social class with which he identified. He dealt neither with the painful social problems his country was facing after achieving unification nor with the tragedy of living in wretched and often hopeless conditions.

The seven novels Fogazzaro wrote are uniformly set in genteel milieus: the villas of the affluent north, principally in the Veneto region, where he was born and reared; in the Turinese halls of the Italian Parliament; in the fashionable German, Swiss, and French spas. We move, in short, in the cultured, morally spotless world of the bourgeoisie, imbued with noble feelings, liberal in its politics if conservative in its outlook on social questions. Fogazzaro's characters are oversensitive, sophisticated almost to the point of being decadent, well-read, musically gifted, and capable of discussing difficult points of religious philosophy, politics, and ethics. In this one respect at least the novelist was both original and even ahead of his time. Writing in an era of realism and naturalism, and himself affected by the prevailing concern about the effects of science on social and moral mores, he strove to compose a narrative with a discernible ideological content. He created characters for whom the discussion of ideas was an integral part of their lives, even though a closer examination would reveal that it remained a kind of ornament, a façade without real reason for its being. Intellectual as Fogazzaro's heroes are meant to be, they strangely engage in little debate on a high ideological plane. It might well be that ultimately culture for them was but a means to render their lives more palatable and interesting, lending them a style they would otherwise lack; yet, it is also true that it is their intellect that supposedly generates what might well be called the chief element of tension in the dramas they enact, the struggle between their senses and their spirit. As they are presented to us, they seem preoccupied by an inner conflict that springs from a doubt: the doubt that the discoveries of the new science will ultimately shatter the validity of their religious beliefs to which they have always tenaciously clung. They are therefore destined to be tormented and torn by their doubts, and lead a life that being a mixture of eroticism, patriotism, and mysticism is further confused by the approximate solutions they find to the riddles of their existence.

"At the center of his novels," writes Gaetano Trombatore, "is love: a love romantically ideal, but neither innocent nor insipid, [either] contaminated by the sharpness of the sexual desires to which it feels irresistibly attracted, or otherwise pushed toward the particular state which gave it birth in order that it may maintain itself pure." Fogazzaro's novels read almost like splendid catalogs of neurotic loves: there is the love of a woman for a man who only resembles someone who died long ago, there is the love for a woman other than a wife and repressed to the point of forcing the hero (Piero Maironi, *Piccolo mondo moderno* [*The Little World of the Present*]) to seek spiritual refuge in a monastery; there is Daniele Cortis' love for his cousin, Elena, shabbily treated by a vulgar husband, and there is even love for a dead man. However many the situations may be, we are always treading on the dangerous borderline dividing sin and innocence, for the love that attracts the Fogazzarian hero is one that torments, corrodes, leaves no time for tranquillity of mind and of the body—nothing less than a devilish temptation.

During his particularly productive and unusually comfortable life in pleasant surroundings, amidst friends and admirers, blemished by few sorrows, rich with official recognition of his talent, Fogazzaro wrote several novels, the last of which (*The Little World of the Present, Il Santo (The Saint)*, and *Leila*) form a trilogy and are loosely connected with the events of his recognized masterpiece, *The Little World of the Past*.

As P. M. Pasinetti succinctly put it in his recent assessment of that book, "the standard evaluation of *Piccolo mondo antico* is that this one novel represents the moment of happy balance between thought and image, between the debating of ideas and beliefs on the one side, and the authoritative presentation of flesh-and-blood characters and moving events on the other." The linear, uncomplicated plot of the book, its ideological unpretentiousness, enabled the novelist to avoid making some of the glaring mistakes marring his other works. But even his best work has traces of sentimentality, romantic mysticism, and a preoccupation with the supernatural and the occult that is seldom artistically realized.

The Little World of the Past is set in Vasolda, between the years 1852 and 1859, during a period which was poor in events though rich in conspiracies and underground activities aimed at subverting the existing political order. The tale it tells, against the background of the Risorgimento, is one of love, the love and marriage of Franco Maironi and Luisa Rigey, two young, patriotic likeable people whose diverse temperaments eventually bring them to a conflict that nearly breaks up their marriage. Neither the historical component nor the love story, however conspicuous a part they have in the book, may be said to be self-sustaining. Fogazzaro uses them as devices to explore a theme close to his sensibility: the dramatic confrontation between two opposite views of life. Differently from Manzoni, however, whose *The Betrothed* seeks to demonstrate the validity of a Christian way of life and of man's faith in Divine Providence, the events of Fogazzaro's novels are contrived only to prove his point. In sum, and this is a realization we reach when Fogazzaro's novels are exam-

ined in retrospect, they are constructed a priori, not with
the intention of following the way his heroes change,
evolve, and mature—through their actions, their mistakes
and doubts, their involvement with reality—but of demonstrating the correctness of his position. In such circumstances, there can be little real drama in his novels, since
surprises and changes are denied to people whose positions
are stubbornly fixed.

The locale of the story Fogazzaro felicitously described
as "the little world of the past," where the mail was
delivered three times a week, where the inhabitants spent
their leisure time fishing in the tranquil waters of Lugano,
dreaming of their eventual deliverance from the oppres-
sors, and planning their customary evening *tarocchi*
games. It is an old world, carefully observed, where a
political system is about to collapse—a collapse that threatens even traditional religious beliefs. The world is painted
by Fogazzaro in muted, restrained colors that contrast
with the black and white he uses to create his characters,
neatly and conviently divided into two groups: the honest, decent, good Italians pitted against the hated, tyrannical, cruel Austrians. The novelist's inability to concentrate
on the nuances that make people so similar and yet so
different is carried into the ideological conflict that looms
large in the tale. There is, we finally sense, something a
trifle boring about people who are as cut-and-dried as
Franco and his old, marble-cold grandmother, who can be
moved only either by religious dogma or political "appetite."

Yet the real subject of the book is the nature of the
special relationship between Franco and Luisa, crucially
determined by respective conception of justice, which is
religious in the former and tragic in the latter. Fogazzaro
himself, in a letter to a friend, touched on this aspect of
his novel in these words: "She [Luisa] lives for this world,
not in the sense of enjoying it; in the sense, rather, of pity
and justice exercising themselves *here* without preoccupations about the other life (in spite of the apparent religious practices). *He* lives, in theory, for the next world,

but in practice for the present one—to enjoy it, not badly, but honestly." The confrontation that takes place is only apparently religious. Luisa, in fact, is unable to accept her husband's ineffectual role as an intellectual who dreams of, and longs for, his country's liberation but is unwilling to fight for it; she sympathizes even less with his failure to earn a livelihood for his family and translate his vague belief in justice into some kind of a program of action. No sooner are the two married, than they seek shelter in the home of Luisa's uncle, the engineer Piero Rebeira, who finds himself persecuted and eventually fired from his job through the machinations of Franco's grandmother (who sides with the Austrians since they represent the power capable of preserving the *status quo*). Franco's position is made still more difficult by the opposition of his grandmother (who holds the pursestrings) to his liberal and mildly revolutionary ideas and to his marriage with Luisa. The novel moves along a line of events that permit the author to test the relevance of the individual moral positions of his heroes and to show in which way they are able, thanks to their respective philosophies, to cope with the human and political crises they meet.

The central, crucial event that serves as *the* test of their strength is the sudden death of Maria, nicknamed Ombretta Pipí by her uncle, the couple's precocious and beloved child, who drowns in the lake while her father is in a self-imposed exile in Turin and her mother is about to face Franco's grandmother and denounce her wickedness and dishonesty. As the story makes plain, the misery and abjection the two are forced to endure could indeed have been avoided had Franco been disposed to resolve the question of the will left by his grandfather naming him his heir. Despite the fact that the will was never properly executed (thus leaving Franco to his resources, his grandmother's whim, and his uncle's charity), the hero stubbornly clings to his refusal to take legal action against his grandmother, partly because he does not intend to ruin the family reputation, partly because he loathes her money, but above all because of his instinctive superior charity that is the foundation of his moral standards. Thus the problem of the book comes to a head with Pipí's death, which takes place at a moment when each of her parents is, in a real sense, practicing his special version of morality. Through his religious faith, Franco succeeds in finding the strength that will sustain him in the hard months ahead. Luisa, on the other hand, first refuses to accept the fact that Ombretta Pipí had died, then turns against God, whom she accuses of having unjustly taken her little girl away, and finally resorts to occultistic practices through which she hopes to make contact with the soul of her dead child. Franco not only weathers the storm, but decides to take a more active role in the struggle for his country's independence and enlists in the Piedmontese army. Only at the end of the book are the two reunited, shortly before Franco is to leave for the frontline as war against Austria is now imminent. When the story comes to a close, we know that Luisa has returned to life: she will bear another child, and her union with Franco is, once more, spiritually and physically complete.

From even such a bare outline of the plot of the novel, it is clear why the confrontation between Franco and Luisa is easily resolved in his favor, for it is conception of a superior justice that is deemed ideologically better than his wife's stubborn, yet strangely contemporary view that if justice is to exist at all, it must be cherished, upheld, and above all practiced in the everyday experiences and activities of man.

Simply stated, and like the overwhelming majority of nineteenth-century Italian novelists, Fogazzaro did not conceive of the novel as an art form whose purpose is to illuminate the human condition while at the same time entertaining in the best sense of the term, but rather, as a mode that would permit him to identify and fictionalize his moral, religious, and patriotic ideas, translating them into virtuous teachings that would ultimately improve man's character. He worked from his imagination and from his personal experience; he drew from the political life of his era as well as from the morose, morbid imaginings of his fantasy. He believed in certain values—God, the family, the country, the necessity of work—yet he depicted characters, whose values are questionable at best and unrealistic and inconsistent at worst; what is even more deplorable, he created them with an astonishing incapacity to face life and resolve with the desired success the very problems posed by existence.

Admired in the past, but not fashionable today, *The Little World of the Past,* with its simplicistic view of life, its easy solutions to complex religious and moral issues, remains of some interest to those who wish to find, represented in fiction, an image of a world that is no more, and to those who seek in it an idea of how a novelist viewed the historical events of his generation. When all is said, however, the befogging answers given by the novelist, his partial interpretations of history, his implacable bourgeois point of view, are bound to embarrass more than to please, to confuse more than to illuminate the human condition. Yet, it would be foolhardy to neglect him simply because he is no longer responding to our interests and curiosity and seems to have become suddenly, but not inexplicably, old-fashioned. Despite all the flaws of his fiction, the superficial manner in which he ideologized his novels, he remains, by and large, one of the finest examples of the effort made by the bourgeoisie to believe in a time when all beliefs were questioned and debunked; to evaluate its spirit in times of decadent morals; to strive toward a nobler existence. To a considerable extent, his failure as an artist was the mirror of the failures of his class and of his nation.

9 ITALO SVEVO'S ANTIHEROES

AMONG NINETEENTH-CENTURY Italian novelists, it would be difficult to find one whose curriculum—his education, upbringing, experience, and literary career—is as unorthodox as Italo Svevo's, the *nom de plume* of Ettore Schmitz. Born in December, 1861 (the year marking the official unification of Italy), in the northeastern city of Trieste, a busy harbor then under the enlightened rule of the Austro-Hungarian Hapsburg family, Svevo spent a considerable part of his life first at the desk of the Triestine branch of the Austrian Bank Union, and subsequently in the busy office of a marine paint firm of which he was part owner. By virtue of his birth, he found himself living in a city that, geographically and culturally, occupied a peripheral position in Italian life, semiforgotten by all except the most enthusiastic *irridentisti* (who clung to their dream of an Italy that would include Trieste), prosperous in commerce and unusually cosmopolitan in its culture. It was a background that, as we shall soon see, was to play an important role in shaping the novelist's sensibility and interest.

During a lifetime spent primarily as a business man, Svevo found time to complete three major novels, several short stories, occasional journalistic pieces, and a still-uncertain number of poems and plays. He also left sections of novels in progress, quite clearly intended to complete his earlier work. He was literally discovered in the early twenties by Eugenio Montale, the hermetic poet who was destined to become the unofficial spokesman of an entire generation (the generation of T. S. Eliot's *The Wasteland*), and quickly won the accolades of Benjamin Crémieux, Valéry Larbaud, and his own friend James Joyce, whose affection and esteem had been instrumental in making possible Svevo's entrance into the sophisticated literary circles of Paris. The critics unanimously praised Svevo, calling him a brilliant artist, possibly one of the finest Italy had produced in the first part of our century, and underscored the boldness and uniqueness of his world view. Today, we are struck less by the originality of Svevo's characters, or the realism of his novels, than by the urbanity of his approach. Not only did Svevo fictionalize a world whose anxieties we have to recognize as our very own, but he strikingly departed from conventional narrative techniques by exploiting the psycho-analytical findings of Freud and by employing what we call the stream-of-consciousness method.

There is an extraordinary element of irony about Svevo's life. Born into an ordinary middle-class family without intellectual pretensions, he grew up to become one of those remarkable novelists with whom every serious student of fiction must reckon sooner or later. Aspiring to greatness, he remained largely ignored during his lifetime. When, at long last, he succeeded in gaining international attention, and the ensuing recognition and fame, he was unable to savor his hard-earned success. He died in an automobile accident in 1928, joining the ranks, as someone pertinently put it, "of those great modern writers who are very much regarded but very little read." By another twist of strange destiny, Svevo became one of those rare artists who are esteemed abroad even before they can be appreciated in their native country. Translated widely, praised by an ever-growing audience of readers, almost three decades after his death Svevo continues to be a large enigma (or "problem" as critical jargon in Italy would put it) for most of his countrymen, who have recently begun studying him seriously not merely in the history of his own culture, but as a vital force in European literature.

Why should Svevo be a problematical figure for Italian critics? The question may be partly answered by looking somewhat more closely at the nature of his opus. Unlike his contemporaries, Svevo refused to be overburdened by linguistic or stylistic questions—this by itself places him in a special category in a nation so deeply conscious of the refinements of poetic language. Few would deny that Svevo's novels are written in the kind of gray, monotonous style most Italians, fervent admirers of *la belle page*, find repugnant to their ears. Although Svevo's prose is highly controlled, in that it demonstrates a capacity to make important statements or unfold the story with great economy of means, it is also static, lacking that dramatic, highly personal flair which distinguishes, for better or worse, the majority of Italian narratives of the same period. Yet, the style is nothing if not the real measure of the man that was Svevo and the artist in him. Even allowing for his unusual preparation as a novelist (particularly his geographical-cultural situation and his trilingual upbringing), it must be conceded that Svevo made a deliberate choice of the language that, in his mind, could most appropriately translate into literary images and events his special world. Interested as he was in the substance, rather than the appearance of things, it follows that his approach would be of the analytical and not of the descriptive kind. This may explain why his narrative is precise, without being overburdened with details; or why it is unpretentious to the point of seeming almost unpoetical (in Italy poetry has invariably been associated with stylistic refinement and virtuosity), or, finally, why it loses little of its essence when translated into another language. The nature of the man also holds the clue as to why he should so frequently employ irony, or ironical statements, in his work, since he saw in irony an apt instrument that would permit him to lay bare his profound skepticism about human nature. He used irony as a kind of oblique weapon that makes evident the incongruity, as well as the humor, of his characters. Examples are abundant, but it may suffice to remember here how Alfonso Nitti (*A Life*) plans to write a philosophical treatise (after deciding that "he would lay the foundations of modern Italian philosophy by translating a good German work"), and how soon enough "the translation remained pure intention" as he never goes beyond writing the first four pages of the preface. Later on, dissatisfied with the progress made by his own work, he plunges "into reading a bibliographical journal" a fact that convinces him of his inadequate grasp of Italian.

By the same token, and again unlike his contemporaries, Svevo eschews anything more than a momentary concern with either the religious or the socioeconomic facets of the human experience. What absorbs him, is the unpredictable behavior of people facing situations that touch vividly on their emotions (or on their sexual drives) rather than on their material needs—people largely unaffected by political, religious, or even ethical problems. The atmosphere he skillfully conjures up in his fiction is not one likely to prod the reader to take sides in the peculiar kind of struggles of created characters—as is often the case in the bulk of nineteenth-century fiction—but rather impels him to watch, with a dispassionate, and almost clinical attention, how men living under the most normal circumstances make themselves look silly or incoherent, and how thoroughly they succeed in wrecking their lives. As represented in his fiction, man is no arbiter of his destiny, no pilot of his course, no hero of a gigantic drama that takes place, day in and day out, on the earthly stage. He is merely a creature who acts instinctively and impulsively, groping for happiness but achieving only misery, knowing himself to be basically insincere, incompetent, and insecure yet striving, or at least pretending, to achieve worthy goals, a badly needed, firm personal relationship with human kind and even moral rectitude. The irony is all in that contrast, in what they *are* and what they *long* to be, if only in their imagination; in the pleasures and victories they seek, and in the anguish and defeats they are doomed to suffer, more at the hands of their own ineptitude than of fate. "I'm ill!" shouts one of Svevo's early heroes, Alfonso Nitti. And the narrator hastens to add that

This conclusion was reached after he had made a series of observations about himself. The deep gloom which turned everything gray and dull for him had seemed till then a natural result of his discontent; his insomnia he thought must be due to nervous tension brought on by night study; and an abnormal restlessness he sometimes noticed in himself must come from the fact that his muscles and lungs were insisting on exercise and pure air . . . now he was constantly, monotonously, obsessed by one vision which made him incapable of taking part in the present, hearing and examining anything said by others.

What may shock us about the world of Svevo is that it either does not know or refuses to point out evil or good, right or wrong. "Evil just happens, it is not committed," states Emilio Brentani in *Senilità* (New York, n.d.; *As a Man Grows Older*). The author adds: "In that tumult of waves . . . he read the impassivity of fate. No one was to blame for that destruction." No one, that is, except ourselves. The pervading feeling we are bound to get from Svevo's novels is of an absurd, incoherent world, where man is prevented by his self-deception, vanity, egotism, false idealism, and spineless character from taking cognizance of his own frailties, and is even less able to share his happiness or sorrows with others.

To penetrate the reasons for this sad state of affairs, the novelist turns his focus not on reality, but on the human consciousness. Much of his work is so constructed that it allows a sustained look at the contradictions between reality and personality, what we would like to see and what we must acknowledge *is*. In the last analysis, this is the secret of his modernity, the reason why the contemporary reader can turn to his work and find not the history of a certain period poetically reflected, but the human character brilliantly and amusingly analyzed. There is no doubt Svevo realized that if a poet has the obligation to lead his public to a more complete understanding of the human predicament, a good novelist must also be, in a special way, a great entertainer.

There are other reasons why Italian critics have the right to feel uneasy or annoyed by Svevo's work, so obviously un-Italian to the point of seeming to belong to another culture. I suppose that the diverse nature of Svevo's novels and their general orientation are the elements that set them in a category (or class) of their own. Thus, at a time when *verismo* had reached its zenith, Svevo was writing highly introspective novels, all of which, although clearly set in Trieste, make scant use of the regional backdrop. What we see of Trieste, in short, is not only occasional but never elaborated through factually precise descriptions. More than seeing the city, we feel it, especially and most lucidly when it is used to give added color to the dramatic unfolding of character. Just as Svevo shows an unusual lack of interest in the use of scenery, so he remains largely unconcerned with a mystical approach to life (as Fogazzaro) or with D'Annunzio's superman. But there is still more. Although the novelist felt deeply Italian, despite his obvious ties to Germany, he never overtly expressed in his fiction his views on the political fate of his country, nor his hope that his native city might some day be reunited with the rest of the nation. In a nation prevalently Catholic, he was one of the most areligious writers of modern times; in a culture where the majority of writers, major and minor alike, sooner or later take a stand on the *questione della lingua*, Svevo maintained a consistent aloofness from what many rightly regard as one of the most crucial and burning literary problems.

In other ways, too, Svevo professed little or no interest in those issues of life and culture, of politics and society that his contemporary fellow writers found important or fascinating. He does not dramatize religious or moral conflicts springing from carnal desires, as in Grazia Deledda's novels or as in many of Verga's memorable short stories; nor does he attempt to paint vast, ambitious canvasses of social conditions of certain depressed southern regions—as had been the practice of Matilde Serao, Salvatore Di Giacomo, and a score of realists and regionalists. Nor does he strive for the kind of historical-political tableau so admirably done by Ippolito Nievo and Federico De Roberto among others. His heroes invariably come from the comfortable bourgeoisie, generally untroubled by the necessity of having to work for a living, and not under the strain of having to worry constantly about an uncertain tomorrow. But not everything—indeed, preciously little—is well with the middle class, and his characters live forever under the haunting awareness of their failures and psychological malaise. Yet, all this does not turn Svevo into a social reformer, much less an utopian. What makes him an appealing writer for today's readers is his undisputed acceptance of the condition of sickness pervading the world, transforming it, as Richard Gilman acutely remarked some years ago, "into the condition of existence itself, making uprootedness, alienation, moral uncertainty and social weakness—as opposed to unseemed and coerced integrity—into agencies of wily enduring and liberating instruments of self-knowledge." The Svevian hero likes nothing better than the excruciatingly relentless, if often unproductive, self-analyses to which he subjects himself, for through such self-examinations he achieves a human dimension. For him, one can well repeat what the novelist says apropos Alfonso Nitti: "Self-knowledge made him suffer." Perhaps out of his desire to avoid a direct confrontation with himself coupled with his incredible incapacity to cope with the complexities of life, he discovers the usefulness of his illness—an illness that invariably has all the symptoms of a psychosomatic disorder. Because they are ill (one thinks here of how sickness has sharpened the sensitivity of poets of all generations, from Tasso to Leopardi, from Simone Weil to Moravia), they are overconscious of how people react to what they say or do. Indeed, their malady, as yet undefined, visibly increases their sensibility, even if what they feel is invariably a distortion or a rationalization of the real reason for their malaise. It is not without justification that Angiolina, the heroine of *As a Man Grows Older*, despite her dubious morals, is depicted as a woman enjoying good health, even if her behavior toward her lover is bound to seem perverse in that it is calculated to bring Emilio Brentani an unusual amount of misery. Good health, we must assume, means simply a *joie de vivre*, the ability to let oneself savor whatever little life has to offer, without worrying about repercussions, moral values, or implications from whatever quarter they may come; it also means to come to terms with oneself and accept oneself as one is, limiting our goals or adjusting them to conform to our abilities.

As it has been hinted, the reality Svevo observes and describes, with a method that in its calculated meticulousness leaves nothing to the imagination, is quite limited. The eyes of his heroes, or of his narrator-protagonist, scan a landscape that is possibly one of the narrowest in modern Italian fiction. Only when the landscape serves to illustrate, reflect, or dramatize the psychological state of the characters, are we allowed to see it. Svevo's technique, in fact, permits him to create a story with a maximum of dramatic content with a minimum amount of attention to external reality. To be sure, this is the way it should be, not only because the life and experience he narrates are gray and monotonous, but because his tales are turned inward, bent on discovering the mechanism of the human personality, the nature of passions, the discordance between our goals and our possibilities. As a consequence, one cannot expect to get from Svevo a feeling of society, nor much less a sense of history unfolding before our very eyes, as in Manzoni, or in historical novels and *veristic* tales. The air we breath in Svevo's novels is more rarefied than that of most of his contemporaries; in a limited sense, it evokes that of Tozzi's silent, gloomy Sienese countryside; likewise, the tensions Svevo creates have something of the electric quality of G. A. Borgese's fiction.

If in his choice of themes, or in his structural innovations, or in his slow-moving style Svevo shows himself to be a kind of outsider, it is to certain other sides of his work that we must turn to discover his uniqueness. I have already mentioned his obsession with psychological illnesses; I must now add his engrossing concern with ennui. For it is boredom—so vividly dramatized by as contemporary a novelist as Moravia in a book bearing the appropriate title *La noia*—that is one of the great forces of Svevo's universe. Leopardi and Baudelaire recognized it as such in their poetry, and Svevo exploits it to the utmost in his fiction, where it becomes the condition that encouarges introspection. Thinking about oneself can be a dangerous affair; in the world of Svevo it forces a reexamination of the whole question of self-fulfillment. Can man, living in a world laden with frustration and absurdities, achieve the capacity of doing some of the things he knows, deep in his heart, he is incompetent or unfit to do? Manzoni might have answered this question in religious terms, and Verga in economic ones. Svevo, on the other hand, along with Pirandello and Moravia, felt that if an answer does exist, it must be sought in ourselves, in the very depth of our conscience. Nonetheless, as a writer, Svevo concerned himself not with finding answers, but in exploring this and other facets of the human condition; not in preaching, but in dramatizing the dilemmas of modern man, living in a world where standards have suddenly collapsed; not in attempting to extend his range horizontally, but vertically. His truths may be few; but they are, in the main eminently vaild.

In terms of his personal life, there are a few additional elements that may be useful to understand his work. When he was quite young he was sent to a Bavarian school at Steignitz, near Würzburg, because his father was convinced that a German education was essential in those days of Austrian control. Svevo's encounter with the classics of German and European literature took place then. Shortly after the return to his native city, at the age of seventeen, he was enrolled in the commercial institute Pasquale Revoltella. A serious setback suffered by his father's business forced Svevo to interrupt his education and find a job. He was hired as a clerk by the Union Bank, where he spent the next eighteen years. Far more important than the practical experience he gained at the bank, where he achieved a measure of success through his industriousness and seriousness, is the fact that his continued exposure to the world of finance and bureaucracy allowed him to acquire definite insights into the petty intrigues and shabby existence of white-collar employees. It was largely this experience that inspired him to write his first novel, *Una vita* (New York, 1963; *A Life*).

Seven years after his marriage to Livia Veneziani, in 1892, he entered the firm of his father-in-law; once more, he fictionalized his experience in his third major novel, *La coscienza di Zeno* (New York, 1958; *The Confessions of Zeno*) written after an unusual silence that lasted two and one-half decades, no doubt caused by the poor reception his previous literary efforts had met.

It is impossible to pinpoint accurately the factors that impelled Svevo to entertain literary ambitions. His letters and personal confessions to his friends and associates reveal only that as a youngster he manifested the desire to become a writer, and received the encouragement of one of his brothers. His first published writings, however, were not fiction or poetry, but criticism. For some years, between 1880 and 1890, he was a regular contributor to the Triestine newspaper *L'indipendente*, then edited by Giuseppe Caprin. His reviews of plays and books are intelligent and well informed, if hardly inspiring. As can be expected, their chief value rests in their indications of the novelist's cultural preparation and taste, and they may be considered accurate barometers of his opinions and postures with regard to European literary trends and movements. Taken together with his letters to his wife, his articles throw some light on his cultural formation. His readings consisted primarily of the work of French realists and naturalists, Flaubert, Stendhal, Balzac, Zola, de Maupassant, as well as Daudet, Renan, and the philosopher Schopenhauer.

Already in the days of his schooling in Germany, he had had the opportunity of dipping into German poetry—especially Goethe, Schiller, and Heine; it was only somewhat later that he became acquainted with the great nineteenth-century Russian playwrights and novelists, Gogol, Tolstoy, Turgenev, and Dostoyevsky. Traces of these and other writers may be found in his own writing, less as direct sources than as suggestive forces. Svevo's heroes move and brood in a manner that recalls the Russian novelists; and, in a manner that will certainly call Flaubert to mind, Svevo presents his characters without ever making an explicit act of judgment. In his view, in fact, all men are equally guilty and equally innocent and deserve to be absolved; living itself, so he implies, is sufficient punishment for any wrongdoing human beings may commit.

He completed his first novel in 1892, but that event did not bring him particular joy. "[This book]," he wrote "will end up sticking in my throat." Strangely enough, he continued to regard it with affection throughout his life and even considered it his best work. He was twenty-eight at the time of its inception, and already considered himself a failure insofar as his literary dreams were concerned. The themes of failure and of creativity are frequently interwoven in Svevo's novels, and time and again his heroes have distinct artistic ambitions. Alfonso Nitti, the hero of *A Life*, for example, is a would-be philosopher, who entertains the plan to write a treatise on "The Moral Idea of the Modern World," a project that never gets off the ground; subsequently he agrees to write a novel in collaboration with the daughter of the bank's director, Annetta Maller, with whom he has fallen in love. That project, too, becomes the excuse for some hilarious scenes. Similarly, Emilio Brentani, the protagonist of *As a Man Grows Older* is a published writer whose first work has earned him the esteem of the local cultural circles. When he takes up his pen again, to compose another novel inspired by his disastrous love affair, he is unable to go beyond the first few pages and gives up. Finally, Zeno (the hero of *The Confessions of Zena*) writes his memoirs as a therapy that will supposedly enable him to overcome the psychological malaise which afflicts him. For Svevo, writing is an activity best pursued by those who, although employed, have the interest and time to devote to thought about themselves. Svevo's heroes, in fact, never seem to be under the usual pressure of having to earn a livelihood, a situation most conducive to brooding upon and verbalizing their problems. With the single exception of Nitti, no job occupies more than a small part of a Svevian character's time, since the normal pursuits of man—working, raising a family, etc.—are only of peripheral importance in his day. Nitti has a clerical post in the Maller Bank; Brentani is an insurance agent (but that and little more is all we are given about his position); Zeno, after a rather inconclusive life, becomes the partner in his brother-in-law Guido Speier's import firm, whose success is due less to their personal ability and good management than to fortuitous circumstances that surprise them as much as they surprise us. In this respect Svevo merely follows the pattern of a bourgeois writer for whom the traditional concern with earning sufficient money to take care of today's needs and tomorrow's uncertainties is not compelling enough to warrant more than casual attention.

Svevo's first work, *A Life,* brought out at his own expense after it had been turned down by several publishers, contains the first intimations of a new turn in novel writing. Structurally and thematically, the book is pretty much anchored in the narrative tradition of its years, being, in a sense at least, a *tranche de vie,* a life—I hasten to add—of the most undramatic kind. The novel opens with a letter written by its hero, Alfonso Nitti, to his mother, who lives in a small town, and it ends with a dry, official communication addressed to Luigi Mascotti by the Maller Bank announcing the unexplicable death by suicide of the protagonist. The drama of Svevo's bourgeois character—the prototype of Moravia's and Camus's uncommitted and indifferent heroes—is contained between the two letters. Superficially, the letters are used as devices, obviously borrowed from the tradition of French naturalism, for the purpose of documenting the story, perhaps to lend further credibility to it. Both letters, however, manage to do more than that. The first may be read as a statement of dissatisfaction with the situation in which Alfonso finds himself in his first encounter with city life, and with the puzzling aspects of a life he is apparently unable to comprehend. This letter is the first clear evidence of the insecure temperament of the hero (riddled, as we shall see, with anxieties) and an anticipation of the long list of disappointments caused both by his ineptitude and by his lack of direction. His central disappointment, if we are to believe his letter, stems from the failure of those among whom he lived to appreciate his intellectual qualities. The suicide, announced by the final letter in the impersonal style of a big business firm, may be understood in terms of the protagonist's inability to make contact with his colleagues and superiors, his incapacity to take stock of himself and accept his own incompetence—as a worker and as a man—as the real factor that has denied him the necessary strength to overcome the tough battles of life. In another sense, the tone of the final letter points up even more the inconsequential character of everything that has taken place in the book, and denies the human element of what can hardly be called a tragedy.

All this tends to make *A Life* a narrative less concerned with showing us Alfonso's vain attempts to make good in the big city, than with a subtle representation of a humdrum life among the white-collar class, the robot-like nature of a society where man frequently aspires only to an imitation of other lives, an empty repetition with no feeling and involvement. The hero is a distinct failure not because he has no interest in succeeding but because he is incapable of doing like the others and hence achieving his goals. Thus, while Svevo originally intended to write a novel of customs and manners patterned after the work of Balzac, Flaubert, and Zola, the finished product comes closer to being an absorbing, if somewhat uneven, study in the psychological key of the failure of a man without consequence, a kind of Robert Musil's *Man without Qualities ante litteram*. Perhaps here is the first notable feature of the book: written with the narrative modes of the realists and naturalists he admired so fervently, it creates a climate not of a city but of a way of life whose dominating

traits are futility, boredom, and senselessness of purpose—the unmistakable flaws of the twentieth-century
bourgeoisie. In a universe without values where love, patriotism, honor, and compassion are either unknown or
slighted by its inhabitants, everything is part and parcel of
a great illusion no longer believed. In the cosmos of Svevo,
man has ceased being an active participant in the historical process and has accepted the passive role of silent
spectator to the decay of the social and moral code of his
country and of the world. In a situation of this sort man
usually resorts to seeking or creating new goals which will
give him renewed importance.

Svevo attacks the problem from two angles. First, like
all good naturalist writers, he hints that the cause of man's
ineffectuality and failure is to be found in his environment. Then, with a subtle twist, he demonstrates palpibly
that it is lodged in the mind of the individual. Action and
descriptive passages are skillfully exploited by the author,
not to spin a plot but to develop and reveal character. We
do not become acquainted with the personages of the
novel through the comments and remarks of an omniscient author, but through the shabby behavior and dou-
ble-edged reflections of the characters themselves. When
the prose is precise, it inevitably conveys the meticulously
orderly world of the Maller Bank; its attention to details,
however, hints at the unauthentic quality of the people
who work within its walls. Theirs is a life of routine
movements, of superficial human relations, of petty goals
that underscore an existence without aspirations and hope
of substantial changes. It is in such a dismal milieu that
people like Alfonso, or White, or Luigi Miceni, are
doomed to exist.

> As six o'clock finished striking, Luigi Miceni put down his
> pen and slipped on his overcoat, short and smart. On his
> desk something seemed out of order. He arranged the edges
> of a pile of papers exactly in line with the rim of the desk.
> Then he glanced at the order again and found it perfect.
> Papers were arranged so neatly in every pigeonhole that
> they looked like booklets; pens were also at the same level
> alongside the inkpots.

This passage, of course, depicts with painstaking accuracy the uninspiring life led by the bank's employees, as typified by Miceni, and creates an apt atmosphere at the same time. But again and again Svevo uses descriptions not merely to provide tangible points of reference for the tale but to give us perceptive reflections of, and insights into, his characters. Moreover, in the blunt, sordid world of a civilization where documents and appearances are thought to be of such importance, it is easier for men to arrange the order of things than that of their souls, or that of their moral universe. Luigi Pirandello will echo such a preoccupation in his fiction and theater, although he will do so with a greater metaphysical intensity but with a far smaller psychological precision. Svevo's world, even if it is imperfectly represented in his first novel, exhibits an impressive inaction that prevents much horizontal movement. His is a world where people do not feel deeply about one another, and much less, entertain noble concepts about their human destiny. "This is precisely the fundamental tragic character of *A Life*," notes A. Leone de Castris, "small gestures, whispered words, small thoughts enveloped by a scabrous, fatal atmosphere . . . [Svevo's] creatures do not hope, do not love, do not sing, do not smile." The most serious sides of life—pain, love, work, hope—can no longer be taken seriously, and are purposely played down by the novelist, who gradually robs them of their human content, frequently reducing life itself to a quasi-caricature. To put the situation in a metaphor, Svevo's characters seem to live in a spiritual wasteland surrounded by nothingness, incapable of sharing their few joyous moments with anyone, all equally condemned to an insufferable mediocrity.

Alfonso considered himself to have poise. In his soliloquies he certainly had. Having never had a chance of displaying this quality to people whom he considered worthwhile, now, on his way to the Maller's, he felt as if his dream was about to come true. He had thought a lot about how to behave in society, and prepared a number of safe maxims to take the place of long practice. Speak little, concisely, and if possible, well; let others talk, never interrupt, in fact, be at ease without appearing to make any effort. He intended to show that a man could be born and bred in a village and by natural good sense behave like a poised and civilized townsman.

What we find ourselves confronting are often not real people, but make-believe men and women—so much so that if we understand them we are frequently unable to sympathize with them. In the case of Alfonso Nitti we soon perceive that there is nothing in his temperament that even remotely justifies the unusually high opinion he has of himself, or the intelligence he thinks to be his chief asset. When the duties normally assigned to him at the office become more onerous, he proves to be incapable of discharging them, or of demonstrating his leadership and imagination unless he is coached by his fellow worker White. By the same token, Alfonso's ambition is to become a writer, yet he reads novels "still having a boy's contempt for the so-called 'light' literature." His training and education seem to be based largely on a treatise of rhetoric, whose theories he absorbs as he dreams of "becoming a writer who would unite good qualities and be immune from the bad ones." When the time comes at last for him to begin his literary career in earnest, he agrees to cooperate with Annetta Maller in writing a novel. The work they are to write together turns out to be a futile exercise that brings poor Alfonso humiliation and despair, for he is forced to tolerate Annetta's ridicule and scorn for his efforts. Their meetings, during which they read each other's pages and subject them to mutual criticism, become eventually but excuses for the two to find the proper circumstances for their lovemaking. Soon enough, in fact, Annetta proves to be the weaker of the two (after having been merciless in her reproaches of Alfonso's work) and is seduced by her literary partner. Even then, however, Alfonso is unable to understand the nature of his feelings toward her, or to perceive how she envisions their relationship, and is therefore incapable of exploiting the situation to his own advantage. He takes an emergency leave of absence, claiming that his mother is ailing and needs him.

By coincidence, his mother is very ill and dies during her son's visit. Her death could hardly have come at a more appropriate moment, and Alfonso, who had invented his mother's illness to resolve his predicament, does not have to justify his absence from the office and avoids a confrontation with his mistress' brother who has challenged him to a duel. Alfonso fares no better with Lucia Lanucci, the young daughter of a couple in whose house he has rented a room. While she is absolutely charmed by him and admires his intelligence and education, he remains totally blind to her longing for affection. Unaware that she is simply not suited for studying, he insists on educating her by giving her grammar lessons. So much does he exasperate her that at one point she hurls three insults at him that fittingly reflect the reader's own judgment of his behavior up to that point: "Fool, idiot, donkey!"

It is unfair to categorize Alfonso as a stupid individual, however, because if this were true the novel would certainly lose much of its poignancy and pathos. He is willing to acquire a certain cultural sophistication, though the reader will find it a bit grotesque that Alfonso goes to the library to read criticism he does not understand and a bibliographical review written in Italian, a language with which he is still unfamiliar! No matter how desperately Alfonso strives to learn the ways of the world, the strange art of living in a society whose rules he does not comprehend, he fails miserably. The main trouble is that he lacks the stuff that makes for the kind of individual he would like to be. Only "in his dreams," Svevo notes at one point, "he was capable of heroic action." His predicament is further compounded by the fact that he spends all his time and energy preparing himself for a life yet to come, realizing neither the vacuum within him or his lack of creativity, yet another evidence of his utter incapacity to seize the opportunities that periodically present themselves to him. "Alfonso," writes Svevo early in the novel, "knew French but his ear was not attuned, so he found it difficult to understand." *Mutatis mutandis* is a statement that applies to life as much as it does to his French. His failure is acknowledged in the final paragraphs of the book simply yet pointedly: "He felt incapable of living. Some feeling he had often tried and failed to understand made it an unbearable agony to him. . . . He knew neither how to love nor how to enjoy. . . . He was leaving life without regret. It was the renunciation of which he had dreamed." But if such thoughts are expressed only as the story comes to a close, and as Alfonso is ready to turn on the gas to take his life, the reader has had ample chance to observe the special situation of the hero at close range: "He is like a mouse," observes a critic, "turning round and round in a wheel." It is a senseless merry-go-round, an incredible exercise in futility that springs from a special type of malaise from which all Svevian heroes suffer: "He talked feelingly of an illness which he could not define, a disquiet which took away sleep, pleasure in study, joy in life; everything bored him." Unprepared to face life, Alfonso has no alternative but to renounce living.

Such are the themes of Svevo's first novel—themes that reappear in the following novels and that make plain the fact that our writer is primarily concerned in creating the unusual world of frustrations, defeats, and anxieties. To be sure, however interested Svevo is in the psychology of his hero Alfonso Nitti, it is clear that *A Life* is definitely oriented toward a palpable, and hence easily describable reality. In his first two novels, the author accepts the convention of chronological treatment, while slowly moving in a direction that will see him become increasingly fascinated by the possibility of analyzing the motivations that often secretely or unconsciously generate activity or passivity in man. Part of his interest also is in a constant conflict between the stuff of dreams and the stuff of reality, which is at the root of his characters' inability to comprehend fully the nature of their predicament until it is too late to really matter.

If the whole first novel revolves around the common incidents of the life of a clerk, *As a Man Grows Older*, Svevo's second book, is a tale where a minimum amount of attention is given to anything that does not directly concern the special, and most unusual, relationship between the two central figures.

In *A Life* we found ourselves moving in a world of things, of business affairs and petty machinations, a world whose characters achieve at times a comic stature. By contrast, *As a Man Grows Older* is far more direct than the first novel, has fewer characters, and exhibits a narrative manner that is at once sophisticated in its focusing on the sentimental life of its protagonist and illuminating in its analysis of the hero's malaise. The protagonist, Emilio Brentani, is a refinement and an extension of Alfonso Nitti. His predecessor was primarily concerned with succeeding in business and in life, and was ready to blame society for failures that could only be attributed, in the last analysis, to his own ineptness. Emilio is exclusively concerned with the possibility of savoring, as the book carefully tells, everything that he had missed up to now. His past life, incredibly devoid of passions, loves, disappointments, or ambitious plans, he considers as a mere preparation for the period of happiness that awaits him. His practical situation is succinctly summarized by Svevo with these words: "Emilio Brentani's career was a more complicated matter, because at that time it consisted of two distinct occupations, with completely diverse aims. His official career was a quite subordinate post with an Insurance Society, which was just sufficient to provide for the needs of his small family. His other career was literary, and apart from the mild degree of fame, which flattered his vanity rather than satisfied his ambition, it brought in nothing, but also took nothing out of him." The remark may seem casual and almost innocent, were it not for the strategic position it occupies in the very first chapter of the novel. The earlier paragraph which opens the book presents the protagonist (as yet unnamed) proposing to a woman that she become his mistress on the condition that she be considered no "more than a plaything." Emilio specified that he has "other duties in life, my career and my family." His family, as we immediately discover, consists of a spinster sister "who made no claim at all on him, either physically or morally." His career is described in the paragraph that follows, and which I have cited earlier. A colorless clerk without a past—such is the hero of the book. A would-be writer, perhaps under other circumstances, who has already completed his creative cycle; his major problem is that, unwilling to give to life, he must therefore resign himself to expect nothing. The rest of the book will demonstrate just how a woman can be a plaything, and how a career only incidentally important literally destroys whatever chance of happiness Emilio might have had.

Svevo launches the story *in mediae res*, with no preparation whatsoever, and with a remarkable briskness thrusts his hero into a predicament from which he will have considerable difficulty extricating himself. Brentani insists that the harmony of his life not be disturbed; his love affair will bring him a physical and an intellectual pleasure. For years, in fact, Emilio's pen has been idle. Now, "under the inspiration of Angiolina's blue eyes," things will change. Poor Emilio is simply too naïve to perceive that "plus ça change, et plus c'est la même chose." Before reality can change, man must change.

No amount of action will be able to radically alter anything. Here, once more, is what makes Svevo a fascinating novelist to watch for his tale is relatively poor of events. We feel attracted to it not by the plot but by the slow unfolding of character and motivations. We notice how the author relies on a subtle irony to create a special kind of suspense and an overt, amusing contrast between what Emilio chooses to see and what, in a real sense, *is*. Thus, for example, Emilio "as a preparation for her [Angiolina's] initiation into vice, assumed the severe aspect of a professor of virtue." Little does Emilio suspect that Angiolina Lazzi, for such is the name of the "tall, healthy blonde, with blue eyes and a supple, graceful body, an expressive face and transparent skin glowing with health" for whom he has fallen, is far from being the angel her name implies. Not only does she have an extraordinary experience in the ancient art of love, but she is frequently surprised (as we infer from her actions) by Emilio's naïve attitude. Despite the incontrovertible evidence that keeps accumulating against his stubbornly romantic notion of her purity, Brentani persists in clinging to the idea that Angiolina is a woman deeply in love with him. When he eventually is forced to admit to himself that she has had numerous affairs in her young life, he agrees to her having other men (one of whom has ostensibly promised to marry her) so long as his own libidinous passion is satisfied. Page after page, we follow the disintegration of the myth of Angiolina as a simple, modest, honest girl from the working class and her transformation (always observed and described indirectly from the side, as it were) into a personable whore. Yet, her immoral behavior increases, rather than decreases, our sympathy for her. Her unconventional sexual behavior is more than compensated by her zest for life, her unrestrained, joyous sensuality, the disarming way in which she continues to deceive her lover and resist all efforts made by Emilio to change her into what she is not, cannot, and has no wish to be. Emilio's moralistic plan to change her—or, better still, to mold her into something that will more completely suit his convenience and his desires—is but another facet of Svevian heroes, all of whom have the zeal of a reformer, the pedagogical pedantry of a teacher, the narrow-mindedness of a sterile clerk, and the empty loftiness of an idealist obviously out of touch with the world. They all share a disquieting incapacity to realize that they live in a world made intolerable not by nature, but by human egotism that aims only at self-satisfaction.

As a Man Grows Older differs in a number of important ways from the earlier book. Its cast of characters, far smaller than that of *A Life*, permits the author to pay greater attention to the development of the relationships between Emilio, Angiolina, Stefano Balli (the hero's only friend and in many ways his mentor), and Amalia. Every element that would distract the reader from a more total understanding of such relationships is carefully avoided. Scant attention is given to descriptions of locales as devices to build up climate, although on a number of occasions Svevo adroitly uses the weather to reveal or intensify our knowledge of the characters' moods and states of mind—always perceived psychologically rather than lyrically. As in A *Life*, there is an antagonist (the sculptor Balli), whose chief role is to guide the protagonist toward the road of self-knowledge. The characters are purposely paired off; on the one hand, we have Emilio and Angiolina; and on the other, Stefano and Amalia. In the first case, it is the woman who causes pain to her lover; in the second, it is the woman who, in love with Stefano, is doomed to loneliness. A weak man (Emilio) balances a strong woman; and a strong man (Stefano) balances a weak Amalia. Emilio is in love with Angiolina and Amalia secretly loves Stefano, but neither of these two loves will be returned. If Emilio does manage to learn a limited lesson out of his unfortunate love affair, the disillusionment will actually drive Amalia to alcohol and drugs which will hasten her death.

In yet another way, As a Man Grows Older marks a further withdrawal from the real world of the business circles in which Alfonso Nitti lived: in the second novel we find ourselves less concerned with the state of things than with states of mind. The affair we are allowed to contemplate, objectively yet closely to the hero's consciousness, involves middle-aged Emilio Brentani, who realizes he has permitted life to pass him by. The problem is that Emilio insists on living his days as though they were his last on earth. As the curtain is about to descend on the final act of the drama we call life, it is possible to recognize the meaning of what had been a series of events, and see them as part of a larger pattern ordained by God or Fate. But Emilio is content with assuming the posture of an old man (hence the justification of the title *Senilità*) without possessing the maturity and wisdom we normally associate with old age. He is thus unable to savor the pleasures of the moment, cherish the memories of the past, or look with courage to the future and becomes an inept, confused man, whom no real experience, however shattering or traumatic, can really touch. He is satisfied with reminiscing about his past, remaining immersed in a continuous process of changing his experience of life into poetic images that are only barely connected with reality.

At the age of thirty-five, the desires for pleasures he had never tasted, for love he had never known, surged up in his heart, but with a sense of bitterness and frustration at the thought of all that he might have enjoyed; and he was conscious, at the same time, of a great mistrust, of himself, and of the weakness of his own character which hitherto he had had occasion rather to suspect than to prove by actual experience.

The masterful description, all the more effective because of its brevity and candor, gives us more than a hint of Emilio's yearnings and his flaw, the uncertainty that corrodes his temperament and condemns him to a perennial condition of inferiority hardly conducive to a stable or sane existence. Svevo's hero, ill-prepared and ill-suited for the adventurous life he desires, must thus remove the stuff of life from its proper setting, and place it in his imagination where everything is by necessity more tranquil since it does not conflict with anything. As Mr. Pholf intelligently points out, "For Emilio and his spinster sister, Amalia, past moments are subject to reinterpretation, not to reenactment. Emilio is able to embellish their content intellectually and in retrospect, but not to re-enter and tangibly re-fashion that content." Nothing much can be of avail to the hero under such circumstances, and Emilio's "essential characteristic [is] to delight in evoking the sentiments of the past" brings him little relief and no happiness whatsoever. His life at the office (in one of the rare moments when we are reminded of his real occupation) becomes "more and more trying. It cost him a great effort to devote sufficient attention to his work. He took advantage of every pretext for leaving his table and spending a few more moments in nurturing and caressing his grief." Finally, after the whole frustrating love affair with Angiolina can be considered finished, Emilio transforms his experience into reverie.

Despite its title, the novel is not the tale of an old man but of a state of mind portrayed in its full concrete dimensions. In a real sense, as A. Leone de Castris hints, the hero is experiencing "a progressive crumbling of his youthful restlessness to the point where it reveals itself to be incapacity and failure." It is in that formula that we find the essence of the Svevian hero: his incapacity to experience any of the human emotions (one thinks here not only of Emilio Brentani, but of Alfonso Nitti as well), or his experiencing them in a manner and at a time out of tone with his physical age. In *As a Man Grows Older* we are led to a more total understanding of the reasons leading to Emilio's failure. We discover that his aloofness from life and his lack of love for it are essentially to blame for the anguish he experiences during his troublesome liason with Angiolina. To be sure, Emilio is afforded numerous opportunities to become involved with all kinds of people—friends, associates, relatives. Yet, as is invariably the case with Svevo's heroes, his encounters never manage to become meaningful confrontations that may add to his experience or transform him, even in his premature old age, by giving him a new dimension, new opportunities to develop himself, and opening new vistas over the barren life he knows. His coming together with people, his growing appetite for new experiences (experiences, one must add, that ultimately contribute nothing to his development as a person because he learns nothing from them), his adventures, sordid as they might be, never materialize into anything genuinely important. They remain superficial contacts, not vital connections capable of stirring the inert sea of his consciousness, and therefore leave nothing at all after the unimportant storm that momentarily disturbed his peace of mind has passed. As the author remarks at one point, "Emilio had himself never inspired any strong emotions, be it love or hatred." Like the bulk of Svevo's personages, he starts with nothing and ends with nothing, eager to forget, rather than to come to grips with, and be enriched by, experiences that have brought him to the threshold of new knowledge about the quality

of the human heart. Once again, the pattern of his predecessor Alfonso is repeated, as Emilio is described with
these words: "He had understood nothing, heard nothing,
and was even incapable of worrying. He went slowly off to
his place, taking short steps so as to gain time and interrupt his beloved vision as little as possible." Since he has
learned nothing from his disastrous experience, he is
hardly capable of making even the necessary complete
break with his mistress. The only way he can manifest his
pent-up resentment is to hurl some pebbles after her in
what is certainly one of the most effective scenes of the
book: "The wind carried them along, and one must have
hit her, for she uttered a cry of terror. The others struck
the dry branches of the trees and produced a sound which
was ridiculously out of proportion to the anger which had
raised his arm to throw them."

Incapable of feeling, and much less of living like a man,
content to transform life into images through which he
may relive, in his memory, everything that he had not
been able to savor in reality, Emilio truly exhausts his
possibilities when the two chief reasons of his life, Angiolina and Amalia, are no longer part of his existence. Only
years later Emilio succeeds in changing what had been a
lurid chapter of his life into something that is ideal and
beautiful.

> Years afterwards [Emilio] looked back with a kind of en-
> chanted wonder on that period, which had been the most
> important and most luminous in his life. He lived on it
> like an old man on the memories of his youth. Angiolina
> underwent a strange metamorphosis in the writer's idle
> imagination. She preserved all her own beauty, but acquired
> as well all the qualities of Amalia, who died a second time
> in her. . . . He saw her before him as on an altar, the per-
> sonification of thought and suffering, and he never ceased
> loving her, if admiration and desire are love. She stood for
> all that was noble in his thought and vision during that
> period of his life.

In the last analysis every one of Emilio's acts has been a
fruitless attempt to give life a vitality it lacked to make it

more palatable and even more exciting. Yet, an empty life can bear no flower; thus the tale must end anticlimactically. Amalia dies and at last Emilio can start living again. In his mind he creates an ideal picture of his mistress as he would have liked her to have been, a mixture of the sensual mistress he had and the moral, luminous, quiet beauty of his tender deceased sister.

Death, old age, and sickness—mainly of a psychological kind—coupled with a creative impotence form the dominating preoccupations of Svevo's novels. The question of failure also looms large in his tales, a failure that stems from the hollowness of the protagonists, from their incapacity to perceive that only by changing internally can they become more productive, perhaps more successful, certainly less frustrated individuals, unburdened by anxieties. Typical, in this respect, is the author's impassive characterization of this state of mind *vis-à-vis* Emilio's special reason for wanting to reestablish a liason with his mistress.

> The reason he wanted to try and see Angiolina again was that he might try to acquire a certain warmth of thought and speech which he was lacking within himself, and which he must supply from the outside, and he perhaps hoped to live the novel he found himself unable to write.

Curiously and obstinately, the heroes of both of Svevo's early novels strive to find something in life, something clearly beyond their reach, that will permit them to intellectualize and order the meaningless course of their existence. By contrast, the protagonist of *The Confessions of Zeno* not only refuses to become engaged in what would surely be a frustrating quest ("What is life?" "What can man do to fulfill himself?") but indeed abandons himself entirely to the unpredictability of life and ends by winning the skirmishes that had defeated his predecessors. In Zeno's case, it is impossible to apply a statement Giorgio Luti makes about Emilio Brentani: "The cycle of life is concluded by the absence of desire." Zeno Cosini never gives up satisfying his desires, whether they be a marriage, a mistress, a successful business or, last but not least, his smoking. He even succeeds in writing a highly amusing work of fiction—for he is the author of the book—and hence attains what had remained for Alfonso Nitti and Emilio Brentani an unfulfilled literary ambition.

Many are the elements that are bound to strike us about this enigmatic and complex novel: its "significant randomness and outward formlessness" (in the definition coined by Lowry Nelson, Jr.); its pungent irony; its seemingly casual pace; its comic episodes; but, above all, the wonderfully funny way in which everything that happens is the result not of calculated design, of intrigues and plottings, but of pure chance. Thus, for example, the woman Zeno marries is not the one he had chosen, but the one who has been almost saved for him. Having met the Malfenti family and having fallen in love with Ada, he proposes to her but is gently turned down. Quite logically (for Zeno has indeed a personal logic that defies analysis), he proposes to Alberta, only because she is alphabetically next in line after Ada. Finally, he settles for Augusta and finds peace and even happiness in his unusual marriage.

Unlike the two previous novels, written in a traditional chronological manner, *The Confessions of Zeno* is in the form of a diary, but a diary written in retrospect, and therefore in a manner that will allow its author to make a choice between what is and what is not to be included in the book. Several chapters make up the work—six in all—and they are preceded by a brief Introduction and a Preface that outlines the purpose of the confession. The Preface, however, is written not by Zeno, but by Dr. S., the psychiatrist who has decided to punish his patient by publishing his diary written for therapeutic purposes. "Write away!" Dr. S. urges Zeno, "and you will see how soon you begin to get a picture of yourself." The trouble, as Svevo readily acknowledges through Zeno, is that "a written confession is always a lie." What Zeno can give us through his book is but a distorted, partial, and highly selective account of the main incidents of his life which, had they been given by a more detached observer, might conceivably have produced a meaningful picture of the causes and results of the special malaise afflicting the hero. Like his predecessors, Zeno feels the impelling need to justify himself, and draw, as it were, a balance sheet of his life now that he has reached the enviable period of maturity (at least in a chronological sense, separated as he is from his childhood "by over fifty years"). This is possible to him because he has the kind of perspective denied to Alfonso Nitti, who had chosen death over life, or to Emilio Brentani, whose experiences are the direct result of a state of mind peculiar to an old man. Differently from either of his two predecessors, Zeno Cosini proves to be a true genius in telling the story of his life (and what a story it is!). The events of his existence are presented in a highly controlled manner which purposely predetermines our reactions to and interpretations of his actions. The structure of the book while undoubtedly somewhat puzzling is considerably more contemporary in that the central events of the protagonist's life (or at least, those events *he* considers central) are chosen not according to the conventional criterion of time sequence but of actual importance in shaping and explaining his neurotic personality.

There are other reasons, too, why Zeno's remarkable diary is closer to our sensibility than its actual date of composition would make us suspect. The careful reader, especially if he is aware of the tradition of what might well be called the confessional genre (which counts such towering figures as St. Augustine and Dante among its practitioners), realizes that the book, as conceived and realized by Zeno-Svevo, is actually a perversion of a serious attempt to lay one's life bare before a jury (we, the readers), charged with the task of examining it and passing judgment on it. No critic has analyzed this side of the question with greater perspicacity and an equally rigorous preparation in mediaeval art better than John Freccero, and no one has made a better case for the futility of Zeno's attempts. "For the Middle Ages," writes Freccero, "in order to make one's confessions (or write one's confessions), one needed a point in Being in the stream of becoming. Such a point could only be provided by grace. . . . The miracle could be brought about by God who had Himself died and been reborn. . . . But Zeno's funny attempt to stop smoking, which is presumably his search for conversion to a 'new life,' is an act of bad faith, for his self-accusation, like Rousseau's and like that of the man from the underground, is in reality self-justification. Zeno's frustration is the ironic proof of the fact that in Svevo's eyes, such a conversion is impossible in human terms. . . . Zeno looks everywhere for his moment of truth except within himself." Perhaps this is the reason why, as Freccero points out, Svevo should actually indulge in what is a parody of Dante's autobiographical book, *The New Life*, and of its emphasis on dates which are pregnant with allusions to the Trinity. Unlike Dante, however, Zeno never moves in a journey of metaphysical and religious change. Unable to transcend this life, to reach out for a truth that is above and beyond living man, he simply acknowledges, "I remember everything, but I understand nothing." He is, in this special sense, the epitomy of modern man, left to solve the riddle of existence, and to find new values that somehow may enable him to find the quietude of heart without God. "Now that I am old," reflects Zeno, "no one expects anything of me." He is thus absolved of any further responsibility regarding his future actions, and he pleads for compassion for having so irresponsibly groped for life's meaning and significance. The world is asked to reconcile itself to Zeno's whims, to his weaknesses and frailties; the world, and we the readers particularly, must simply adjust ourselves to the hero's errors and constant rationalizations.

The structure of the novel is such that it is fruitless to speak of it abstractly. Through the episodes of the book we are given glimpses of varying length, intensity, and interest into Zeno's life. The variety of moods, the depth of perception, and the resulting insights are nothing less than mirrors of life's variety and of the diverse meaningfulness of man's events in it. The achievement of the structure is that, despite its disregard for a linear treatment of the action, it does succeed in developing an absorbing case history of its highly neurotic hero. The book's installments, aside from being slices of Zeno's life and thus serving the purpose of the book—to tell a story —are also eminently ironic demonstrations of how, simply through his uninvolvement, Zeno succeeds in turning disasters into common occurrences and failures into successes. Every chapter has an individuality of its own to the point that it might be read with profit and enjoyment, either singly or as part of an absorbing case history. All chapters are also linked by the one aspect that is central in Zeno's life, his *malattia*. It ultimately makes little difference whether his special illness (what would Svevo's heroes do and be without an illness, real or imagined?) is smoking, an inferiority complex, an incapacity to find a mode of being in an admittedly purposeless existence, the anxiety brought on by advancing years, or just the desire for a mistress. The need is always the same: to give Zeno something to think and be concerned about; to make him more conscious in an artistic sense (by remembering) and in a psychological one (by feeling deeply guilty) of the pivotal episodes in his life that most clearly reveal him for what he has been. Problems for all men can simply be avoided, as Zeno soon discovers, by giving in to human wishes. It is not without importance, therefore, that the novel should begin with Zeno's alleged determination to undergo extensive treatment to rid himself, once and for all, of his *vizio* of smoking. The habit of cigarette smoking is, in fact, revealing of Zeno's character, the very element that gives his existence consistency and coherence, the central illness that explains all his flaws of character. Once in the clinic, Zeno is warned of the special precautions devised to prevent him from leaving the place where he is to be kept under constant surveillance. No sooner has his wife left, however, than Zeno persuades the nurse to let him go back home, as he suspects that his attending physician is actually carrying on with his wife. He pokes fun at what is, if not his most serious, certainly his most interesting and revealing illness—smoking—just as he will, later on, make a mockery of all the institutions, official or otherwise, of life itself: marriage, a son's relationship with his father, the running of a business, his own social life and, in the end, war itself. But in a way, the initial chapter, "The Last Cigarette," is typical of Svevo's own sense of humor and perhaps is his best attempt at buffoonery. The whole episode, from the moment he enters the clinic to his return home (where he finds his suspicions justified, because his wife has moved some furniture and therefore disturbed the *status quo*), reads like a comedy. The episode like the rest of the book is like a crazy graph on which Zeno records his failures and his vain attempts to attain "health." His fruitless motions, however, are lucid reflections of his peculiar style of life, of the way he faces, examines, and resolves (in his own manner) the crises of his existence. It's always the moment for a last cigarette, to be followed shortly by just one more cigarette, which also promises to be the last. The habit, which began when Zeno, as a youngster, strove to imitate his father, persists throughout his life. "My days became filled," Zeno acknowledges at one point, "with cigarettes and resolutions to give up smoking, and, to make a clean sweep of it, that is more or less what they are still. The dance of the last cigarette which began when I was twenty has not reached its last figure yet. My resolutions are less drastic and, as I grow older, I become more indulgent with my weaknesses. When one is old one can afford to smile at life and all that it contains." Temptations prove always to be too great to resist, and Zeno readily gives in to them. Yet the thought that life might have been different had he only succeeded in overcoming his smoking habit haunts him at times: "Who knows whether, if I had given up smoking, I should really have become the strong man I imagine?" The answer to his question is eloquently given by his actions, the special way in which he faces the great questions of his private life—the way in which he conducts himself with his dying father, his wife, his mistress, his business partner (Guido Speier, the man he admires, who marries Ada and ends by taking his own life). What we are given to see, in a succession of scenes ranging from the serious to the grotesque, from the pathetic to the humorous, is a man continually engaged in a process of self-deception, avoiding any and all honest confrontations with his problems, his family, his friends, and himself, perennially rationalizing his shortcomings to the point where they are transformed into something as desirable as his improbable virtues. Zeno's life is lived not according to the dictates of his conscience, his emotions, his feelings; nor is it shaped according to a design most human beings sooner or later envision. It is, in its sum total of failures and successes, nothing more or less than the product of whim and chance. Someone else might have found the situation confusing and, of course, highly disturbing. Zeno, on the other hand, simply lets himself be carried by events and, ironically, his unorganized way of living has a special way of paying dividends. His marriage is the result of unadulterated chance, to be sure, but this hardly prevents our hero from being quite happy with it; by the same token, when his father-in-law, whom he admires greatly, advises him one day to sell a sugar stock that is supposed to take a steep drop in the Bourse, Zeno conveniently forgets what others would consider a previous tip from an expert investor and weeks later he finds himself substantially wealthier when the stock registers a strong advance on the board. Likewise, in his business venture with his brother-in-law, an excellent violinist and apparently a successful husband and lover, it is Zeno who ultimately triumphs. Guido's incredibly poor business judgment, his disastrous speculations, his incompetence eventually drive him to suicide, and it is Zeno, the weakling, indecisive, erratic partner, who not only saves the business from bankruptcy but indeed puts it on the road to solvency and success.

In Zeno's private and public life, one incongruity follows another—and the course of his life is reduced to a series of pseudo-Hamletian questions of whether to smoke or not to smoke, always repeating the pattern of indecision implicit, indeed rooted in and best exemplified by his first problem. He wavers between law and chemistry, between working and not working, and after his marriage he becomes interested (briefly) in religion which, for him "was a different thing. If I had only believed, nothing else in the world would have mattered." He conveniently forgets that if he believed in *anything*, everything else *would* matter. His nonbeliefs, much like his nonaction, are in the last analysis symptomatic of his nonbeing, of a life lived in a purely casual, uncommitted way. In Zeno's world, it is no longer a question of values and worth, but of convenience and vicarious thrills without fulfillment and joy. Typical of this stance is his love affair with Carla Gerco, a would-be singer (without talent), in whose arms he falls like a schoolboy, while remaining also supremely conscious of the fact that his affair increases his already haunting sense of guilt. "Later on," Zeno notes, "when I had really become Carla's lover, my thoughts would go back to that melancholy afternoon, and could not understand why I had not been capable of the manly resolution that would have prevented my plunging deeper in." "Every visit I paid to Carla," he writes, "meant of course that I was unfaithful to Augusta, but all was soon forgotten in a health-giving bath of good resolutions. And there was nothing brutal or sadistic in my good resolutions, as when I had felt a passionate need to tell Carla I would never see her again." In Zeno's scheme of things a betrayal, like a cigarette, is destined to be followed by another betrayal, or another cigarette, and the end result does not change one iota. Even when Zeno is supposed to show up at the funeral of his partner and brother-in-law, and completely neglects to pay his last respects, he is able to persuade his wife and sister-in-law that by mistake he followed the wrong funeral cortege, and thus receives their sympathy and understanding!

It is only in the last chapter of Zeno's seemingly candid confessions, "Psychoanalysis," that many of the novel's perplexing points are resolved with the irony and wisdom truly worthy of an old man who happens to be also an artist. At the end of a long period of association with Dr. S., a period that has been as demanding as it has been revealing, we are given the diagnosis of Zeno's malaise—an Oedipus complex. The reaction of the protagonist is calm and measured: "I did not even get angry. I listened enraptured. It was a disease that exalted me to a place among the great ones of the earth. . . . I don't feel angry, even now that I sit here alone, pen in hand. I can laugh at it whole-heartedly. The surest proof that I never had the disease is that I have not been cured of it." One by one, his ambivalent relations with his father, his brother, Guido Speier, his father-in-law are passed in review, and his attitude toward them varied according to whether they were models he strove so assiduously to imitate, or members of a jury that would inevitably review the course of his existence, a course determined, as many lives oftentime are, by sibling rivalry, an unfulfilled desire to possess one's mother or contempt toward the father figure. "Was it true then that I deserved the blow which my father aimed at me just before he died? I don't know if this was one of the things that he [Dr. S.] said, but I distinctly remembered him saying that I hated the old Malfenti, whom I had substituted for my father. There are so many people who think it impossible to live in a world without a certain amount of affection; but I, according to him, was quite lost without a modicum of hatred." Zeno's reaction to life, with his strange mixture of love and hatred, may well seem ambiguous; but not so is his *malattia*. In his old age, he finds himself afflicted by diabetes, and finds the thought of it "very sweet." "You have talked so much about diseases all your life," comments his wife Augusta, "that you were bound to end by having one." Yet Zeno hastens to add,

> But I loved my disease. I thought with sympathy of poor Copler, who preferred real diseases to imaginary ones. I agreed with him now. A real disease was so simple; you had only to let it work its will. And, in fact, when I looked up the description of my sweet sickness in a medical prescriber, I found a whole program of life (not of death!) drawn up

for the various stages of the disease. Farewell resolutions! Henceforth I should be free of them. Everything would pursue its course now, without any intervention.

I further discovered that my disease was always, or almost always, very agreeable. The invalid eats and drinks a great deal, and suffers very little so long as he is careful to avoid getting abscesses. Then he sinks into a delightful state of coma and dies.

But even this last morsel of consolation is denied to Zeno. A laboratory analysis reveals that he does not, alas, suffer from diabetes, and the news thrusts him back into his loneliness. But we also realize that it was only because of his *malattia* (and this applies to all of Svevo's heroes) that he has preserved the consciousness of his life: "As I looked back over my life and my malady, I felt . . . how much better my life had been than the so-called normal healthy man who, except at certain moments, beats or would like to beat his mistress every day."

And so it is to a life of more lies, of more betrayals, that old Zeno, still under the illusions that somehow sexual love can give him the fulfillment life (but not fortune) has denied him, returns. And it is fitting, as John Freccero remarks, that the lurid—but amusing and engaging—attempts at self-justifications Zeno has called confessions should end, not with the private world of the hero but with a world of universal dimension: the war that brings not destruction but gain to Zeno. And at last war is turned into a concrete symbol of the fact that "our life is poisoned to the roots."

A SELECTED BIBLIOGRAPHY

General Works on Italian Literature

Apollonio, Mario, *I contemporanei*. Brescia: La Scuola, 1956.

Arrighi, Paul, *Le verisme dans la prose narrative italienne*. Paris: Boivin & Co., 1937.

Astaldi, Maria Luisa, *Nascita e vicende del romanzo italiano*. Milan: Treves, 1939.

Avitabile, Grazia, *The Controversy on Romanticism in Italy: First Phase 1816–1823*. New York: S. F. Vanni, 1959.

Bertacchini, Renato, *Il romanzo italiano dell'Ottocento*. Milan: Studium, 1964.

Borgese, Giuseppe Antonio, *Tempo di edificare*. Milan: Treves, 1924.

Capuana, Luigi, *Studi sulla letteratura italiana contemporanea*. Catania: Giannotta, 1882.

Cocchiara, Giuseppe, *Popolo e letteratura in Italia*. Turin: Einaudi, 1959.

Crémieux, Benjamin, *Panorama de la littérature italienne contemporaine*. Paris: Kra, 1928.

Croce, Benedetto, *La letteratura della nuova Italia*. 6 vols. Bari: Laterza, 1943–45. [There are many editions of this work].

Flora, Francesco, *Storia della letteratura italiana*. 5 vols. Milan: Mondadori, 1959.

———, *Dal romanticismo al futurismo*. Milan: Mondadori, 1925.

Galletti, Alfredo, *Il Novecento*. Milan: Vallardi, 1957.

Gargiulo, Alfredo, *La letteratura italiana del Novecento*. Milan: Mondadori, 1947.

Hauvette, H., *Histoire de la littérature italienne*. Paris: Librairie Armand Colin, 1932.

Iliescu, Nicolae, *Il romanzo italiano da Manzoni a Nievo*. Rome: Accademia Romena, 1959.

Kennard, Joseph Spencer, *Italian Romance Writers*. New York: Brentano's, 1922.

Mazzoni, Guido, *L'Ottocento*. 2 vols. Milan: Vallardi, 1956.

Nicastro, Luciano, *Il Novecento*. Milan: Mondadori, 1947.

Olschki, Leonardo, *The Genius of Italy*. Ithaca: Cornell University Press, 1954.

Orientamenti culturali: Letteratura italiana (10 vols.); *Le correnti* (2 vols.); *I maggiori* (2 vols.); *I minori* (4 vols.); *I contemporanei* (2 vols.). Milan: Marzorati, 1956–63. [An uneven collection of essays by various authors on literary movements, trends, major and minor Italian writers, with useful biographies and bibliographies].

Pancrazi, Pietro, *Scrittori d'oggi*. 6 vols. Bari: Laterza, 1946–53.

Pellizzi, Camillo, *Le lettere italiane del nostro secolo*. Milan: Libreria d'Italia, 1929.

Piccioni, Leone, *La narrativa italiana tra romanzo e racconti*. Milan: Mondadori, 1959.

Raya, Gino, *Il romanzo*. Milan: Vallardi, 1950.

Russo, Luigi, *Ritratti e disegni storici*. 3 vols. Bari: Laterza, 1946.

Sapegno, Natalino, *Compendio di storia della letteratura italiana*, Vol. III, *Foscolo ai moderni*. Florence: La Nuova Italia, 1966.

Tozzi, Federigo, *Realtà di ieri e di oggi*. Milan: Alpes, 1928.

Vossler, Karl, *Letteratura italiana contemporanea*. Naples: Ricciardi, 1922.

Whitfield, John H., *A Short History of Italian Literature*. Baltimore: Penguin Books, 1956.

Wilkins, Ernest H., *A History of Italian Literature*. Cambridge, Mass.: Harvard University Press, 1954.

References

Borlenghi, Aldo, ed., "Nota bibliografica," *Narratori dell'Ottocento e del primo Novecento*, I, pp. xcii–cii. Milan: Ricciardi, 1961.

Bosco, Umberto, *Repertorio bibliografico della letteratura italiana*, Vol. I (1948–49), Vol. II (1950–53). Florence: Sansoni, 1953, 1959.

Cordié, Carlo, "Bibliografia speciale della letteratura italiana,"

Questioni e orientamenti critici di lingua e di letteratura italiana, ed. Attiglio Momigliano. Milan: Marzorati, 1948.

Esposito, Enzo, *Critica letteraria*. Rome: Societa Editoriale, n.d.

————, *Rassegna degli studi sulla letteratura italiana apparsi nei periodici del 1961, 1962*. Milan: Marzorati, 1964.

Evola, N. D., *Bibliografia degli studi sulla letteratura italiana* (1920–1934). Milan: Vita e Pensiero, 1938–41.

Frattarolo, Renzo, *Notizie introduttive e sussidi bibliografici*, 2nd ed. Milan: Marzorati, 1959.

Mezzamuto, Pietro, *Rassegna bibliografico-critica della letteratura italiana*. Florence: Le Monnier, 1953.

Prezzolini, Giuseppe, *Repertorio bibliografico della letteratura italiana dal 1902 al 1942*. 4 vols. Vols. i and ii, Rome: Edizioni Roma, 1937, 1939. Vols. iii and iv, New York: S. F. Vanni, 1946, 1948.

Russo, Luigi, *I narratori: 1850–1957*. Milan: Principato, 1958.

Vallone, Aldo, *Bibliografia critica dei romanzieri dalla Scapigliatura all'Ermetismo*. Galatina: Marra, 1945–49.

Selected References

The following is a highly selective listing of essays and books which I found to be particularly helpful and stimulating in the course of writing this book. Whenever possible, care has been taken to include critical material in English.

BACKGROUND OF THE MODERN ITALIAN NOVEL

The most useful historical accounts of Italy in the nineteenth and twentieth centuries are René Albrecht-Carrié's *Italy from Napoleon to Mussolini* (New York: Columbia University Press, 1950), Denis Mack Smith's *Italy* (Ann Arbor: University of Michigan Press, 1959), and Luigi Salvatorelli's *Sŏmmario della storia d'Italia* (Turin: Einaudi, 1950). The literary events of the period treated in the present volume are ably summarized by Aldo Borlenghi in his Introduction to the first of a three-volume anthology *Narratori dell'Ottocento e del primo Novecento* (Milan: Ricciardi, 1961), pp. ix–xcii. The essays "Manzoni e il manzonismo" by Alfredo Galletti, "Il verismo" by Giulio Marzot, and "Il decadentismo" by Francesco Flora in *Questioni e correnti di storia letteraria*, ed.

A. Momigliano (Milan: Marzorati, 1949), III, pp. 659–810 provide a perceptive background for the literary trends and movements of modern Italy. Another good study on cultural and political problems of Italy is by Giuseppe Petroni, *L'attività letteraria in Italia*, 4th ed. (Palermo: Palumbo, 1966). By and large, Italian critics have devoted much attention to individual writers of the modern period, slighting broader questions affecting specific genres. For a recent exception to this approach the reader should consult Carlo Salinari's *Miti e coscienza del decadentismo italiano* (Milan: Feltrinelli, 1960), a brilliant analysis of four Italian writers from a Marxist point of view (especially the chapter devoted to Fogazzaro's *Il santo*, pp. 185–248).

ALESSANDRO MANZONI

The reader wishing to acquaint himself with Manzoni's times and work might profitably turn to two outstanding biographical studies, Alfredo Galletti's *Alessandro Manzoni*, 3rd ed. (Milan: Mursia, 1958) and Archibald Colquhoun's *Manzoni and His Times* (New York: E. P. Dutton & Co., 1954). Barbara Reynolds has produced a scholarly and thorough analysis in *The Linguistic Writings of Alessandro Manzoni* (Cambridge, Eng.: Cambridge University Press, 1950). Giorgio Petrocchi and Angelica Chiavacci have discussed Manzoni's dialogue technique in two works titled respectively *La tecnica del dialogo nei "Promessi sposi"* (Florence: Le Monnier, 1959) and *Il "parlato" nei "Promessi sposi"* (Florence Sansoni, 1961). A comparative treatment of the same question is the essay by Gaetano Ragonese, "La lingua parlata dei *Promessi sposi* e del Verga," *Belfagor*, III, 3 (1948), 288–99.

Manzoni's aesthetics are discussed by Joseph F. De Simone in *Alessandro Manzoni: Aesthetics and Literary Criticism* (New York: S. F. Vanni, 1946). There are three perceptive essays on Manzoni in the European context: Jean F. Beaumont's "Manzoni and Goethe," *Italian Studies*, II, 7 (1939), 129–40; Richard Chase's "Notes on Manzoni's *Promessi sposi* and the European Tradition," *English Miscellany*, XIII (1957), 109–21; and M. F. M. Meicklejohn's "Sir Walter Scott and Alessandro Manzoni," *Italian Studies*, XII (1957), 91–99 (with a useful bibliography). The problem of realism is examined in two books: Mario Bonfantini, *Manzoni e il realismo* (Milan: La Goliardica, 1956) and Ettore Bonora, *Appunti sul realismo dei "Promessi sposi"* (Turin: Gheroni, 1961). Much valuable information about Manzoni and the critical reaction to his work, in his time and after, may be found in Michele Barbi, "I *promessi sposi* e la critica," *Annali Manzoniani*, III (1942), 31–232 and in F. Piemontese, "I *promessi sposi* e la critica contemporanea," *Studi sul Manzoni e altri saggi* (Milan: Marzorati, 1954).

The essay by Moravia, cited in the context of my discussion, may be found in *Man as an End*, trans. Bernard Wall (New York: Farrar, Straus & Giroux, 1966). The impact of Manzoni on later generations of novelists is analyzed by Alfredo Galletti's "Manzoni e il manzonismo," *Questioni e correnti di storia letteraria*, ed. A. Momigliano (Milan: Marzorati, 1949), III, pp. 659–710. Bernard Wall's *Alessandro Manzoni* (New Haven: Yale University Press, 1954), despite the superficiality of its observations, manages to present a rapid analysis of the substance and the important issues of its subject's work.

IPPOLITO NIEVO

Of all minor nineteenth-century Italian novelists Nievo is the one who has most consistently attracted the sympathy of the critics. Of the many monographs on his life and work, it is sufficient to recall here Dino Mantovani's groundbreaking book, *Il poeta soldato: Ippolito Nievo, 1831–1861* (Milan: Treves, 1900, 1932); Mario Marcazzan's *Ippolito Nievo e "Le confessioni"* (Milan: Principato, 1942); and Ferruccio Ulivi's *Il romanticismo di Ippolito Nievo* (Rome: Ave, 1947). C. Bozzetti has produced a thorough review of Nievo criticism, "Le confessioni di Ippolito Nievo e la critica," *Studi Urbinati*, XXVII, 1 (1953), 151–78; while Gaetano Mariani has written a perceptive study, "Nievo e il mondo senza storia," *Letteratura*, IV, 25 (1956), 11–30. In English, there are two fine surveys of Nievo: Olga Ragusa's "Nievo the Writer: Tendencies in Criticism," *Italian Quarterly*, II, 2 (1958), 20–34 and Nicolae Iliescu's "The Position of Ippolito Nievo in the Nineteenth-Century Italian Novel," *PMLA*, LXXV, 3 (June 1960), 272–82. Alfred A. Alberico has published a part of his doctoral dissertation) presented at Yale in 1956) with the title "Nievo's Disquieting Pisana," *Italica*, XXXVIII, 1 (1960), 13–21.

EMILIO DE MARCHI

There are two interesting monographs on De Marchi: the usable *Emilio De Marchi* by Vittore Branca (Brescia: Morcelliana, 1946) and the more recent *Il primo De Marchi fra storia cronaca e poesia* by Marcella Cecconi Gorria (Florence: La Nuova Italia, 1963). For two diametrically opposite estimates of the novelist see the introductory essay to De Marchi's *Opere* by Giansiro Ferrata (Milan: Mondadori, 1959, 1960, 1961) and Folco Portinari's negative evaluation "Bilancio di De Marchi," *Il Verri*, IV, 6 (1960), 7–32. The Introduction by Kathleen Spleight to the English textbook edition of De Marchi's *Il cappello del prete* (Manchester, Eng.: Manchester University Press, 1963) is lively and well informed.

FEDERICO DE ROBERTO

The most recent, and best informed as well as original, interpretation of De Roberto is the volume by Vittorio Spianazzola, *Federico De Roberto e il verismo* (Milan: Feltrinelli, 1961). Gaetano Mariani's slim book, *Federico De Roberto narratore* (Rome: Il Saggitario, 1950) offers several good insights into its subject. Mario Pomilio has written a polemical essay, "L'antirisorgimento di De Roberto," *Ragioni Narrative*, I, 6 (1960), 154–74; while Marcello Turchi has analyzed De Roberto's perspective in "Natura problematica e prospettive storiche dei *Viceré* di De Roberto," *Rassegna della Letteratura Italiana*, anno 64, series VII, 1 (1960), 69–75. The introductory essay by Archibald Colquhoun to the English translation of *I viceré* is particularly valuable.

GIOVANNI VERGA

The best biographical account of the Sicilian writer is the volume authored a quarter of a century ago by Nino Cappellani, *Vita di Giovanni Verga* (Florence: Le Monnier, 1940). Recently, Giulio Cattaneo has produced a valuable though far from satisfactory book, *Giovanni Verga* (Turin: UTET, 1963). From the more critical angle there is Luigi Russo's important, frequently penetrating if at times rhetorical, *Giovanni Verga*, 6th ed. (Bari: Laterza, 1959) and

Thomas G. Bergin's *Giovanni Verga* (New Haven: Yale University Press, 1931). On Verga's style there are two excellent essays, Leo Spitzer's "L'originalità della narrazione nei *Malavoglia*," *Belfagor*, xi (1956), 37–53 and Vittorio Lugli's "Lo stile indiretto libero in Flaubert e Verga," *Dante e Balzac* (Naples: E. S. I., 1952), pp. 221–39. Ines Scaramucci's *Introduzione a Verga* (Brescia: La Scuola, 1959) is a sympathetic treatment of its subject, and Giorgio Luti's essay on Verga (composed of five chapters, originally published in various periodicals as articles) in *Italo Svevo e altri studi sulla letteratura italiana del primo Novecento* (Milan: Lerici, 1961) offers many insights into the style of the Sicilian novelist, the structure of his masterwork, and its position in modern Italian literature. Among the early commentators there is A. Momigliano, *Dante, Manzoni, Verga* (Messina: D'Anna, 1944), pp. 201–59 and Giulio Marzot's *L'arte del Verga* (Vicenza: R. Istituto Magistrale, D. G. Fogazzaro, 1930). The finest piece on "Nedda" and its importance in Verga's development is a short essay by Adriano Seroni, published separately with the same title (Lucca: Lucentia, 1950) and in *Nuove ragioni critiche* (Florence: Sansoni, 1961). Leone Piccioni's essay, "Per una storia dell'arte del Verga," *Letture leopardiane* (Florence: Vallecchi, 1952) is of special interest for its precise stylistic examination of Verga's prose.

MATILDE SERAO

The best biographical study of Serao is Anna Banti's *Matilde Serao* (Turin: UTET, 1965). Banti has also produced a fine anthology of Serao's work with a lucid prefatory essay, *L'occhio di Napoli* (Milan: Garzanti, 1963). For the amusing and tempestuous Serao-Scarfoglio relation see Alberto Consiglio's *Napoli, amore e morte: Scarfoglio e Matilde Serao* (Rome: Vito Bianco, 1958). Michele Prisco has recently written a calm evaluation of the novelist, "Matilde Serao," *Nuova Antologia*, cxxxix, 1838 (1954), 221–36.

ANTONIO FOGAZZARO

For a survey of critical reaction to Fogazzaro one may turn to Antonio Piromalli's volume *Antonio Fogazzaro* (Palermo: Palumbo, 1959). The best biographer of the novelist from

Vicenza is still Piero Nardi, *Antonio Fogazzaro* (Milan: Mondadori, 1945). Raffaelo Viola's study of the writer and poet, *Fogazzaro* (Florence: Sansoni, 1939) is sensitive and sympathetic. Luigi Russo has written two good pieces on Fogazzaro, "L'arte narrativa del Fogazzaro" and "Il Fogazzaro nella storia," found respectively in *Belfagor*, x (1956), 22–36 and xi (1956), 372–92. Maria Luisa Summer's methodical stylistic analysis of Fogazzaro's work, "Le approssimazioni stilistiche di Antonio Fogazzaro," *Giornale Storico della Letteratura Italiana*, cxxviii, 423 (1961), 402–42 and 424 (1961), 522–51, is probably the most brilliant piece published lately. Gaetano Trombatore's "Il successo di Fogazzaro," *Belfagor*, x (1955), 138–49, is a lucid survey from the Marxist point of view. In English, there is the survey by P. M. Pasinetti, "Fogazzaro's *Little World of the Past*: Program Notes for an Italian Classic," *Italian Quarterly*, vii, 27–28 (1953), 3–14. Robert Hall, Jr. has offered a positive evaluation in "Fogazzaro's Maironi Tetralogy," *Italica*, xlii, 2 (1965), 248–59.

ITALO SVEVO

The bibliography on Svevo, while numerically impressive, is qualitatively uneven. There are two monographs on Svevo's life and work: A. Leone De Castris, *Italo Svevo* (Pisa: Nistri-Lischi, 1959), an exhaustive, but seldom clear and direct, analysis of Svevo's literary production; and Bruno Maier, *La personalità e l'opera di Italo Svevo* (Milan: Ugo-Mursia, 1961), a disappointing, superficial analysis of the subject. Carlo Bo, in his *Riflessioni critiche* (Florence: Sansoni, 1953), has written an interesting profile of Svevo, "Per un ritratto di Svevo," pp. 443–64. Giorgio Luti, in *Italo Svevo e altri studi sulla letteratura del primo Novecento* (Milan: Lerici, 1961), has made several vital observations about Svevo's life, cultural background, and themes. One of the most brilliant essays written in Italian is Giacomo Debenedetti's "Svevo e Schmitz," *Scritti critici*, 2nd ed. (Milan: Mondadori, 1955), pp. 50–116. In English, the most penetrating and original piece on Svevo is by John Freccero, "Zeno's Last Cigarette," *Modern Language Notes*, lxxvii, 1 (Jan. 1962), 3–23. Russell Pholf's pages on "Imagery as Disease in *Senilità*," *Modern Language Notes*, lxxvi, 2 (1961), 143–50, are exceedingly pertinent, as are the essays by Edouard Roditi and Renato

Poggioli that serve as introductions to the original American translations of *As a Man Grows Older* and *The Confessions of Zeno*. Lowry Nelson, Jr.'s "A Survey of Svevo," *Italian Quarterly*, III, 10 (1959), 3–33, is a competent piece of work whose value is impaired by the numerous (and frequently unnecessary or questionable) comparisons with other European writers. By contrast, Richard Gilman's review-article, "Svevo: News from the Past," *New Republic*, CXLIX, 18 (1963), 19–23, is an incisively written and unusually revealing study of the quality of *A Life* and of Svevo's importance for the contemporary reader.

For an intimate glimpse of Svevo the man, one must invariably turn to Livia Veneziani Svevo's *Vita di mio marito* (Trieste: Lo Zibaldone, 1951) and *Lettere alla moglie*, ed. Anita Pittoni with an introduction by Bruno Maier (Trieste: Editrice dello Zibaldone, 1963). Livia Veneziani Svevo has compiled a useful pamphlet on *Italo Svevo e la critica internazionale: Rassegna di testimonianze e giudizi* (Trieste: Editrice Libraia, 1956). Additional bibliographical information may be found in Bruno Maier's *Italo Svevo e la critica internazionale*, originally published in *Pagine Istriane*, Nos. 22, 23, 24 (Trieste: 1956). Harry Levin's "Carteggio inedito Joyce-Svevo" (translated by Oreste Pucciani), *Inventario*, II, 1 (1949), 106–38, deals with the absorbing correspondence between the two friends. Giuseppe Pontizzia's article "La tecnica narrativa di Italo Svevo," *Il Verri*, IV, 5 (1963), 150–66, is a careful study of Svevo's technique within the framework of other important European novels.

Montale's correspondence with Svevo, along with his scattered essays on the Triestine, have recently appeared in *Eugenio Montale, lettere, Italo Svevo* (Bari: De Donato, 1966). The essay by Poggioli may now be read in *The Spirit of the Letter* (Cambridge, Mass.: Harvard University Press, 1963). After this chapter had been completed I received the first and only monograph published by an English critic, *Italo Svevo, the Man and the Writer* by P. N. Furbank (London: Secker & Warburg, 1966). The volume contains an excellent account of Svevo's life as well as a penetrating, though brief, analysis of his novels.

INDEX